## Collector's Encyclopedia of

# Old Ivory China

## The Mystery Explored
## IDENTIFICATION & VALUES

*Collection of Muzeum Okregowego Walbrzych, nr inw. MWC – Malgorzata Robaszynska (photo by D. Gdesz).*

Porcelain cutwork platter with center decal of a stylized representation of the Ohme Porcelain works. Piece is from the collection housed at the Okregowe Museum in Walbrzych, Poland.

**Alma Hillman**
**David Goldschmitt**
**Contributing Author: Adam Szynkiewicz**
**Photography: Alma Hillman and Adam Szynkiewicz**

**COLLECTOR BOOKS**
*A Division of Schroeder Publishing Co., Inc.*

The current values in this book should be used only as a guide. They are not intended to set prices, which vary from one section of the country to another. Auction prices as well as dealer prices vary greatly and are affected by condition as well as demand. Neither the Authors nor the Publisher assumes responsibility for any losses that might be incurred as a result of consulting this guide.

## Searching for a Publisher?

We are always looking for knowledgeable people considered to be experts within their fields. If you feel that there is a real need for a book on your collectible subject and have a large comprehensive collection, contact Collector Books.

## On the Cover:

Demitasse pot, "Empire" blank, pattern #123, $400.00.
Tea cup & saucer, Clairon blank, pattern #12, $75.00.
Salad plate, "Empire" blank, pattern #53, $75.00.
Sugar bowl, Worchester blank, $95.00.

Cover design: Beth Summers
Book design: Sherry Kraus

Additional copies of this book may be ordered from:

*COLLECTOR BOOKS*
*P.O. Box 3009*
*Paducah, Kentucky 42002–3009*

@ $24.95. Add $2.00 for postage and handling.

# Contents

# Dedication

For Les, who made this possible.
For Beth, Alan, and Scott, who listened
to endless talk of Old Ivory.
For Doc, who made me believe.
With special thanks to George and Roger.
You kept me going!

*– Alma Hillman*

To my parents for their undying support and love.
To Roger, my backbone and strength.
To Ghislaine, my sounding board and comforter.
To Alma, for putting up with my insanity.
None of this could have been accomplished
without all of you. Thank you!

*– David Goldschmitt*

---

## THE AUTHORS

*Principal Authors:*

### Alma Hillman:

Respected antiques dealer in Searsport, Maine, she became interested in Old Ivory China before it became a truly collectible item. Frustrated by the lack of information available and the confusion surrounding the identification of individual pieces, she set out to enumerate and organize the plethora of materials produced by the Ohme company. In addition to her fund of practical knowledge of Old Ivory and her keen eye, her skill at the difficult art of photographing porcelain pieces has been invaluable in this task.

### David Goldschmitt:

In attempting to organize a ten year collection of Old Ivory China, he discovered the dirth of credible information and the misconceptions surrounding the Ohme lines of porcelains. His organizational skills and literary and historical background provided the impetus for the compilation of the available data and resources.

Bowdoin College — BA art history and biology
University of Chicago — MA divisional masters in sociology
UMDNJ - NJMS — MD

*Contributing Author:* **Adam Syzenkiewicz:**
University of Lodz, Poland — MS geology
Warsaw University, Poland — PhD geography
Presently at the University of Wroclaw: Institute of Geological Sciences — Lecturer

*Polish Liason in the United States:* **Ewa Sienkiewicz**

*Translator:* **Ana Sienkiewicz**

**Alma Hillman and David Goldschmitt**

**Adam Szynkiewicz**

# Acknowledgments

We wish to extend our sincere thanks to all of the dealers, collectors, and others who shared their knowledge, time, memories, and collections with us.

Eleanor Abbott
Vi Baus
Vasco and Marguarette Baldacci
The memory of Dolores Beatty
Jack and Alma Biddlecome
Marie and Richard Bolton
Anna Block
Ruth Brown
Margaret Buck
Anna Canduro
Eleanor Callanan
Gloria and Leon Campbell
Robert Countryman
Myrtle Drew
Tony Daniels
Stephan Elliott
Pat and Dean Fitzwater
Nancy Florian

Joanne Gfeller
Robert Gollmer
Marion Grandchamp
John Harms
Wayne Harp
Margaretta Hays
Cindy Holton
Frances Ivers
Molly Johns
Sig Johnsen
Muriel Knutson
Carl and Jenna Kuttruff
Lydia LaVallee
Marion MacDonald
Mary McDonald
Estell Michaud
Faye Montell
Charles Orr

Bob and Vivian O'Toole
Warren and Gwen Pattison
Nadine and David Ross
Mark Serber
Mabel Slusser
Janice Stockman
Jo and Darrell Thompson
George and Connie Tooze
Weldon and Ann VanPelt
LeRoy Weimken
Charles Wagner
Ed Welch
Jeffery Wainoris
Doug Zea
Ralph and Virginia Wantland
Mr. and Mrs. Dale Zoll
James and Darlene
    Warembourg

A special thanks to Bangor Photo for their invaluable assistance.

Special thanks for information, discussions, facilitations, and consent for publishing all data about OHME porcelains to Pawel Banas, Leszek Nowak, Romuald Nowicki, Jan Sakwerda, Maria Starzewska, Malgorzata Robaszynska, and the Director of the Muzeum Okregowe w Walbrzychu.

The list of those who have helped us in this immense undertaking has been almost too large to count. If we have inadvertently omitted the name of one of you who has aided us in our quest, we extend our sincerest apologies. It in no way means that your help was not appreciated or remembered.

---

Information on the Old Ivory Collector's Club or the newsletter may be obtained from:

**Old Ivory Collector's Club**
c/o John Harms
Box 326
Osage, Iowa 50461

**Old Ivory Collector's Newsletter**
c/o Pat Fitzwater
PO Box 1004
Wilsonville, Oregon 97070

or you may contact the authors directly. In addition, if you are interested in buying or selling Old Ivory China, please feel free to contact:

**ALMA HILLMAN**
Antiques at the Hillmans
362 East Main Street
Searsport, ME 04974

# *Introduction*

Old Ivory China is a collection of delicate and beautiful porcelains produced by the Ohme Porcelain Works in the late 1800s and early 1900s. Little has been known of its origins or history, and, therefore it has been shrouded in mystery. Speculation, theory, and conjecture have led to misinformation and erroneous conclusions from even the most experienced and reliable sources. No literature exists to document the shapes, patterns, or styles of the porcelains. Books on china or china marks barely list this factory, and there is never-ending discrepancy over dates and locations.

What is clear about this china is that a factory existed in Silesia, Germany, from 1882 to 1928 called the Porcelain Manufactory Hermann Ohme. This factory produced two lines of porcelains. The major line was a fine china titled "Old Ivory" after its delicately matted ivory colored background. This finish and color was achieved by china painting the ivory color over the clear glazed bisque and then firing. The second series was a line of hotelware utilizing the same porcelain pieces but finished in clear glaze.

The china was produced in full dinner sets with multiple accessories similar to the Haviland china patterns. Blanks were even given French names as an obvious link to the highly respected French manufacturers. It appears that certain styles of Old Ivory China possessed a more complete line of accessory pieces than others.

The porcelains of Old Ivory and, apparently, the majority of the hotel-wares were produced exclusively for export to the United States. The china was shipped in wooden barrels, often used as ballast in the cargo hold of the ships. The hearsay information provides that the barrels of china were often traded for barrels of fish upon reaching New England, and during the times of embargo of German goods, were smuggled ashore by sailors to trade for desired supplies. With the exception of the area immediately surrounding the factory site in what is now Poland, little or no Ohme porcelains appear throughout Europe. Those that do appear seem to be of the hotelware variety.

There were three major ports of entry of the Ohme porcelains in the United States. The largest import destination was Portland, Maine. The import company of Loring, Short and Harmon appears to be the major distributor from this location. By far, the largest amount of Old Ivory China is to be found in Maine. The second import destination was Boston, Massachusetts. There, the Grayson and Sons import company functioned as the primary agent.

The third port of entry appears to be New Orleans, Louisiana. However, there is no documentation of an importing firm which distributed in that area. Indeed, this area seems to have been the chief import destination for the hotelware. This theory is supported by the amount of clear glazed china which is found in this region as compared to other areas of the country, particularly New England. In addition, several pieces of china bear backstamps which are printed in French.

This dual language marking may represent import preferences for the Creole region of New Orleans.

As previously mentioned, the major port of entry into the United States was Portland, Maine. The china was distributed to retailers throughout the state and surrounding areas. Some of the known places where Old Ivory China was sold were Reddington and Company, Waterville, Maine; M. Simenon at Count and Pascals Grocery, Camden, Maine; Prescot H. Vose and Company, Bangor, Maine; unknown distributor, Bingham, Maine.

It is well known that a large portion of the imported porcelains found their way to the Midwest for retail sales. Particularly the states of Illinois and Iowa seem to have been major destinations. It is well documented that Trask and Plain Jewelers in Aurora, Illinois, as well as a large department store in Des Moines, Iowa, carried the Old Ivory lines. In addition, there appears to have been some interest in the Ohme products in the Pacific Northwest. A fair amount of the china is to be found in Washington state, Oregon, and Northern California.

Old Ivory China was originally marketed in the retail outlets as affordable fine china and elegant dinnerware. At Count and Pascals Grocery in Camden, Maine, dinner plates sold for $1.50 and cruets retailed for $5.00 each. In the 1930s in Bingham Maine, individual pieces sold for $1.00 (the serving pieces were slightly more). The china was promoted to appeal to the same consumers as those of R.S. Prussia and R.S. Germany.

Later, however, it is known that Old Ivory was utilized as free promotional gifts at movie theaters. Perhaps this is why so many small plates and bowls are found today in Old Ivory, as these would be the type given away at a theatre.

Collectors today find this china beautiful and appealing, and slightly more plentiful than originally imagined. It is, by no means, inexpensive, however. The devotee of this treasure must be patient, resourceful, and persistent if one wishes to complete a collection. Hopefully, with the advent of this research, their search will be less frustrating.

The following is the history and origins of this porcelain line as well as a codification and organization of the multiple styles, patterns, and pieces available. The work is by no means complete, but has utilized all of the presently available resources and information.

This matte finished, white glazed small vase in an unknown blank is a commemorative piece. It was produced by the Ohme factory in an unknown year and for an unknown event. The vase encorporates the words "Ohme porcelains," the factory mark, the date of the opening of the factory, and the town (Niedersalzbrunn), into its center decal. The thin gold filigree near the top is punctuated by designs which are reminiscent of the border patterns of Old Ivory China. The piece was located near the factory site in Poland.

# History

## The Man

The owner and originator of the Ohme Porcelain Works was a man named Hermann (or Herrmann) Gustav Ohme. He was born in **1842**, in the small town of Weissenfels a/Saale, which is about **25** kilometers southwest of Leipzig in Saxony, Germany. His parents were Carl August Ohme and Henriette Ohme (nee Fahner).

He spent his youth in Leipzig and enrolled there in a commercial school. As a young man, he apprenticed for a tradesman in Leipzig. The specific training areas or profession in which he apprenticed has not been elucidated.

In 1866, at the age of **24**, he fought as a Prussian volunteer soldier in the Czecho-Moravian-Hungarian war. In **1870 – 1871**, he became an officer in the 72nd Regiment of the Prussian infantry during the Franco-Prussian war. His military experience brought him to the regions of Metz and Dijon.

After the war, Hermann Ohme settled in Hamburg, Germany, opening a small business. This business venture prospered and he gained some financial stability. It is not documented in what area of business his firm operated.

On June **28, 1875**, he married a widow from Waldenburg: one Anna Richter (nee Dimter). She was the widow of August Richter, owner of a prominent gas works in Altwasser, Waldenburg, Silesia. An astute businesswoman in her own right, Anna successfully ran the "August Richter Gas-Works" even beyond the point of her marriage to Ohme.

The Dimter family into which Anna was born was a prominent name in porcelain manufacture in the area. Particularly, August Dimter was an influential name in the field. It is probable that it was through the Dimter family that Hermann Ohme got his start in porcelain manufacture.

In 1881, Ohme officially opened the Porcelain Manufactory of Hermann Ohme in Sorgau, part of Nieder-Salzbrunn, Silesia. Ohme had moved his other business from Hamburg to Waldenburg, where he continued to work in both ventures until **1885**. It is uncertain as to whether he closed the first business at that time, or sold it to an interested party. Either way, from **1885** to **1921**, at the time of his death, he concentrated his interests solely on the Porcelain Manufactory of Hermann Ohme.

From **1885** to **1908**, the family continued to live in Waldenburg. Finally, in **1908**, the house in Nieder-Salzbrunn was completed next to the factory and the family moved in there.

The house is still standing today. It is presently used as a workhouse for young girls. It is named Rodzinka. The address is PL 58-506. ul. Wroclawska (street) 113. Polska.

Ohme had four children from his

marriage to Anna Richter: Joanna Maria Louise, born November 27, 1886; Louise Anna, born April 16, 1878; Hermann Alfred (Junior), born June 16, 1879; and Helene Anna, born June 11, 1881.

Hermann Alfred Ohme Jr. was a chemist by profession, having received his training in Dresden, Breslau, and possibly Bunzlau. Hermann Alfred Ohme Jr. married Katherine Werner and provided Ohme with three grandchildren. They were Lieselotte Anna Helene, born November 21, 1912; Irene Johana Elisabeth, born September 4, 1916; and Hans Hermann Werner Ohme, born October 21, 1921. It is unknown if any of the grandchildren are alive today.

The Ohme family's religion was Evangelist. They, therefore, did not suffer the perils wrought by anti-semetic factions in that area during that time.

From 1906, Hermann Gustav Ohme was a member of the Industrial Artist's Union of Silesia.

In the state archives offices in Wroclaw, there are letters from "Verbund Ostdeutscher Porzellan-Fabriken" signed Hermann Gustav Ohme.

Signature of Hermann Gustav Ohme.

Ohme family house in Nieder-Salzbrunn from northeast view 1923.

View of Ohme family house from north side 1994.

The following is the Ohme family tree from 1842 to 1921 reproduced from the archives of the Taufregister 1911 – 1925, Nieder-Salzbrunn and the Verzeichnis der Gutauften 11/8/78 bis 31/8/81, Waldenburg. Both records are the property and portion of the registry of the Evangelist Church in Wałbryzych.

---

## OHME FAMILY TREE

**Ohme Carl August + Henrietty (family Fahnert)**
**(Weissenfels a/Saale, Saxony)**

---

in Waldenburg
28.06.1875

**Ohme Herrmann Gustav**      +      **Anna Richter (family Dimter**
**born: 1842, Weissenfels**            **born: 1845, Neu Weisenstein**
(see: Arch. Evang. Church in Wałbrzych: Trauregister Waldenburg 61/1875;
Arch. Państ. Wrocław: Standes Amt Waldenburg. Heirats-Haupt Register,
sygn. 8/1875)

---

| Ohme Johanna Maria Louise; born: 27 Nov. 1876 in Waldenburg * no. 33/1877 | Ohme Louise Anne; born 16 Apr. 1878 in Waldenburg * no.413/1878 | **Ohme Hermann Alfred; born 16 Jun. 1979** in Waldenburg * no. 590/1879 | Ohme Helene Anne born 11 Jun. 1881 in Waldenburg * no. 495/1881 |
|---|---|---|---|

+
**Katherine (family Werner)**

| Ohme Lieselotte Anne Helene born: 21 Nov. 1912 in Nieder-Salzbrunn ** no.11/1913 | Ohme Irene Johana Elizabeth born: 4 Sept. 1916 in Nieder-Salzbrunn **no. 148/1916 | Ohme Hans Hermann Werner born: 12 Oct. 1921 in Niedre-Salzbrunn ** no 371/1921 |
|---|---|---|

Courtesy of A. Szynkiewicz 1995

# The Region

The village in which the Ohme Porcelain Works was located has been through many transitions, not the least of which being the transition from Prussia to Germany to Poland over the last 100 years. The town of Sorgau in Silesia, Prussia, is the principal location of the factory. The business offices were located in the neighboring town of Waldenberg in the area of Bezirk Schweidnitz, in the province of Silesia in Germany. The split of countries initially, accounts, in part, for the variety of factory marks on the china: Silesia, Germany, and Prussia.

To further complicate matters, the town of Sorgau is a part of the larger town called Nieder-Salzbrunn (lower Salzbrunn). The importance of the villiage of Sorgau was the location of the Sorgau railway station. In 1945, Nieder-Salzbrunn was renamed Szczawienko and in 1951, it was incorporated into the larger city of Waldenburg, now named Walbryzch.

Nieder-Salzbrunn is situated in the valley of Pelcznica, at the foothills of the northern border of the Sudetes Mountains. The valley is at an elevation of 400 meters above sea level. The valley, and Salzbrunn in particular, was famous in the eighteenth century for health spas centered around mineral springs. From as far back as the fourteenth century, the area was known for the mining of silver and lead. From the sixteenth century, the area capitalized on industrial demands by underground mining of hard coal (anthracite), and the related industries of coking plants and gas works. During the eighteenth and nineteenth centuries, the area was also famous for porcelains and textiles.

The area changed countries frequently. Before 1871, Silesia was part of the Prussian kingdom.

In 1871, the German Empire was formed. From then until 1918, Silesia was a province of the Prussian Kingdom within the German Empire. One can easily see that the factory marks from 1881 to 1918 could contain the names Silesia, Germany, or Prussia. From 1914 to 1918 World War I centered in this area and surrounding regions.

In 1918, the German Empire was replaced with the Deutsches Reich (German Reich). The titles of Silesia and Prussia no longer had significance and, therefore, never appear on pieces produced after 1918. Silesia still existed as a province of the Deutsches Reich until 1945. From 1939 to 1945 World War II again centered in this area and surrounding regions.

In 1945, with the defeat of the German Reich, much of the Reich was divided among the surrounding countries such as Poland and Czechoslavakia. Lower Silesia became a territory of southwest Poland and was renamed Dolny Slask. Many of the cities were also renamed. Breslau became Wroclaw, Waldenburg became Walbryzch, and Nieder-Salzbrunn became Szczawienko.

A further problem in obtaining information is the location of the archives. From 1945 to 1975 Walbryzch belonged to the district of Wroclaw. By 1975, Walbryzch had grown large enough to be a district of its own. The changes in government moved the archives to another location. In addition, a large portion of the older archives from the German Reich were lost in a fire during World War II. Other records are scattered about Germany dependent upon which area was in power during a particular time period.

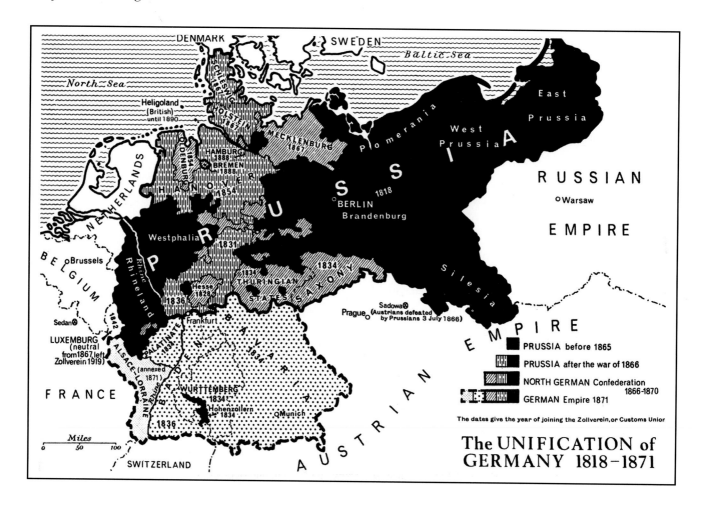

The establishment of the Kingdom of Prussia **1818** to **1871**.

Map of Poland after
World War II (1945).

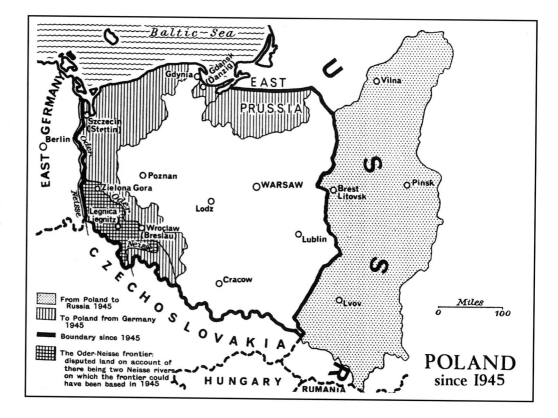

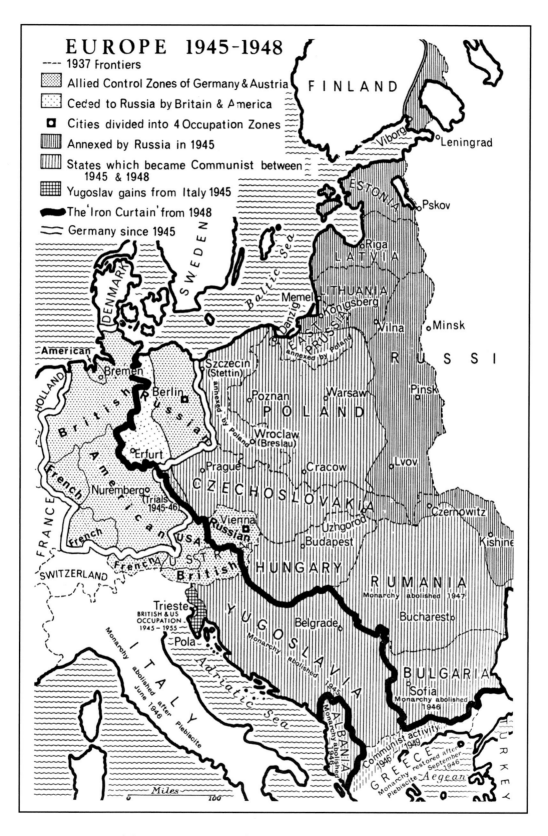

Map of Germany Post-World War II (and surrounding territories).

# The Factory

In 1881, Hermann Gustav Ohme was a businessman in Waldenburg, Silesia, Germany. He and a man named Ernst Maria Bauer, who was an engineer from Sorgau in Nieder-Salzbrunn began the building of a new porcelain manufactory near the train station at Sorgau. Production of porcelains began in 1882.

At the beginning, the factory utilized two large kilns which were fired solely by hard coal. In 1906, Ohme, with the aid of his wife (and her ownership of the August Richter Gas-Works) began to utilize gas fired kilns. By 1917, there were nine operating kilns, some gas and some hard coal. In that year alone, the coal fired kilns consumed 524 tons per month of hard coal. These nine kilns remained in operation until at least 1929.

From 1881 to 1921, the Porcelain Manufactory Hermann Ohme was owned by Hermann Ohme senior. Ernst Maria Bauer functioned as the managing director of the factory for the same time period. He continued after Ohme's death in 1921, but retired in 1923, turning over complete control to Ohme's son. From 1881 to 1908, Paul Stolz, a businessman from Waldenburg was a financial partner in the firm, though it appears that he took no active role in the operation of the factory.

From 1881 to 1893, the manufactory's business office was in Waldenburg. On April 1, 1893, the office was moved to Sorgau in Nieder-Salzbrunn. However, the official main registry of the business and its seat remained in Waldenburg until 1908. On January 1, 1894,

the Porcelain Manufactory Hermann Ohme was officially registered as a company. The seat of the company remained in Nieder-Salzbrunn until at least 1928.

By 1910, the owners of the Porcelain Manufactory were listed as Hermann Gustav Ohme Sr.; Ernst Maria Bauer; and Hermann Alfred Ohme Jr.

In 1923 the sole owner of the manufactory was Hermann Alfred Ohme Jr. By 1927, Ohme Jr. is listed as both owner and managing director.

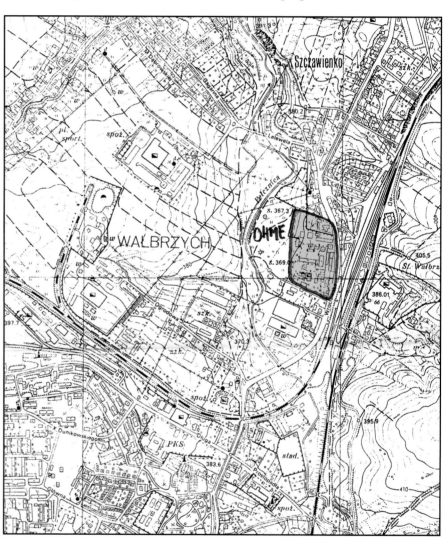

Map with location of Ohme factory buildings in 1994.

Nr. 48.

Waldenburg am achtundzwanzigsten Juni, Ein tausend achthundert siebenzig und fünf — Vor Mittags neun Uhr.

Vor dem unterzeichneten Standesbeamten erschienen heute als Verlobte:

1. Der Kaufmann Gustav Herrmann Ohme
der Person nach bekannt,
evangelischer Religion, dreiunddreißig Jahre alt,
geboren zu Weissenfels, wohnhaft zu Waldenburg und vorher zu Hamburg
Sohn des Kantors Carl August Ohme zu Weissenfels a/Saale und dessen dort verstorbenen Ehefrau Henriette, geborene Fahnert

2. Die Frau Anna Richter geb. Dimter
der Person nach bekannt,
evangelischer Religion, dreißig Jahre alt,
geboren zu Neu Weisstein, wohnhaft zu Waldenburg, Neufreiburgerstraße No. 1.
Tochter des in Neu Weisstein verstorbenen Franz Dimter und dessen zu Schmidsdorf verstorbenen Ehefrau Genofeva geborene Knittel sowie als Zeugen:

3. Der Kaufmann und Fabrikbesitzer Robert Haensitzke
der Person nach bekannt,
sechsundfünfzig Jahre alt, wohnhaft zu Waldenburg Neufreiburgerstraße No. 22

4. Der Fabrikbesitzer August Dimter
der Person nach bekannt,
dreiundzwanzig Jahre alt, wohnhaft zu Waldenburg, Neufreiburgerstraße 8.

Die Verlobten erklärten vor dem Standesbeamten und in Gegenwart der Zeugen persönlich ihren Willen, die Ehe miteinander eingehen zu wollen, worauf der unterzeichnete Standesbeamte dieselben nunmehr kraft des Gesetzes für rechtmäßig verbundene Eheleute erklärte.

Vorgelesen, genehmigt und unterschrieben

Gustav Hermann Ohme

Anna Richter geb. Dimter

Robert Haensitzke

August Dimter

Der Standesbeamte.

Deed to ownership of the Porcelain Factory Hermann Ohme 1882.
Made out to Gustav Hermann Ohme and Anna Richter nee Dimter
as principal owners with August Dimter and Robert Haensitske as secondary owners.

The Ohme factory employed a consistent and large work force for the period of 1891 to 1928. In 1891 there were 326 employees (200 men and 126 women). By 1917, this number had grown to approximately 400.

After Hermann Ohme Sr.'s death in 1921, the factory was restructured under, first Ernst Bauer and then, in 1923, by Hermann Ohme Jr. In 1925 there were approximately 350 employees. By 1927, this number had again risen to about 400. In 1928, at the time that production ceased, there were still 328 employees at the factory.

From 1928 to 1932, there was a deep recession in Silesia. Bearing in mind that the United States, which was the sole export market for Old Ivory Porcelain, was in the Great Depression during the same period, the Ohme factory was affected greatly by these dual financial slumps. In 1928, porcelain production in the Porcelain Manufactory Hermann Ohme was halted. It appears that decoration of existing pieces may have continued until the mid-1930s.

On October 9, 1929, the Porcelain Manufactory Hermann Ohme was sold at auction. The manufactory was purchased by Carl Hamich, a businessman from Alt-Wasser in Waldenburg (though the largest shareholder was a Breslau bank).

In 1932, the Ohme Family house was purchased by Felix Reichert of Waldenburg.

In 1933, part of the land of the Ohme manufactory was purchased by Fraulein Johana and her conservator.

In 1936, part of the buildings of the Ohme manufactory were demolished to harvest the used brick for other buildings. The buildings that survived were the painting house, the Madchencheim Hostel for Girls, a few of the smaller buildings, and the housing for the workers.

In 1938, another part of the Ohme manufactory was purchased by Wilhelm Jung from Waldenburg.

In 1941, another portion of the Ohme manufactory was purchased by Hans Johanes Kube and Kurt Eckert from Gohlenau (near Waldenburg).

The remaining portion of the factory was purchased in 1941 by Franz Riepel of Waldenburg.

During World War II, the factory was used as barracks or caserns for Russian soldiers. After World War II, the factory remained a military base for several years, first for the Russians, then for the Polish Army.

At present, the buildings are used for chemical manufacture and retail stores.

---

**Ausschnitt aus dem „Neuen Tageblatt"**

vom 18./19. April 1936

# Das Ende der Ohmeschen Fabrik
## Umwandlung in Wohnungen / Abbruch der Mittelgebäude

Im Jahre 1928 wurde die Porzellanfabrik Ohme in Nieder-Salzbrunn ein Opfer der Krise. Die Inhaber konnten sich nicht mehr behaupten. Der Fabrikationsbetrieb wurde eingestellt; und das Grundstück ging in den Besitz einer Bank in Breslau über, die es jetzt im Januar mit Ausnahme der erst nach der Inflation erbauten Malerei und des Verwaltungsgebäudes, das von der Gemeinde erworben wurde, an den Kaufmann Karl Hamich in Altwasser verkaufte.

Stillgelegte Werke haben etwas Trauriges an sich. Schon bald zeigen sich Spuren des Verfalls. Jahre hindurch standen die verödeten Fabrikgebäude in bedrückender Zwecklosigkeit, bis der neue Besitzer jetzt endgültig über ihr Schicksal entschieden hat. Die Maschinen wurden ausgeräumt und der Schornstein gesprengt. Die Formen für das Porzellan lieferten 850 Tonnen Gips und 300 Tonnen Schamott, die nach auswärts verfrachtet wurden. Mit dem Abbruch des Mittelgebäudes und des südlichen Langgebäudes wurde schon im Februar begonnen. Man rechnet mit 3 Millionen Ziegeln, die ebenso wie die freiwerdenden Eisenträger und Balken größtenteils zum Bau von Siedlungshäusern verwendet werden. Die Abbruchsarbeiten werden sich noch längere Zeit hinziehen.

Die ganze Vorderfront, die aus drei Häuserabschnitten besteht, soll nach einem vollkommenen Umbau zu Wohnungen eingerichtet werden. Geplant sind 24 Kleinwohnungen mit Stube und Küche, 18 Mittelwohnungen mit 2 Stuben und Küche und 4 Dreizimmerwohnungen. Außerdem werden sich noch mehrere Einzelstuben, deren Zahl gegenwärtig noch nicht feststeht, ergeben. Gas und elektrisches Licht werden in das Gebäude gelegt, 6 Waschküchen und 6 Wäscheböden eingerichtet und 6 Eingänge für die zukünftigen Bewohner geschaffen. Man rechnet damit, daß schon im Sommer die ersten Wohnungen bezogen werden können. Die Hintergebäude kommen wegen ihrer Lage für den Wohnungsbau nicht in Frage. Sie werden später für gewerbliche Zwecke Verwendung finden.

Der Mittelplatz und ein Teil des geräumigen Hofes wird in Schrebergärten umgewandelt und Mutterboden aufgeschüttet. Außerdem sollen ein Spielplatz für die Mieter und mehrere Wäscheplätze angelegt werden. Auch die gärtnerischen Anlagen vor den Häusern werden verschönert werden, so daß sich auch von der Straße aus dem Auge ein gefälliges Bild bieten wird. Die Arbeiten für den Abbruch und für die Umwandlung, die von 40 Mann ausgeführt werden, werden voraussichtlich ein volles Jahr in Anspruch nehmen. fw.

Existing Ohme Buildings

A  Ohme Family house
B  Painting house
C  Madchenheim Hostel for Girls
D  Warehouse or factory building
E  Warehouse or factory building

F  Offices in Nieder-Salzbrunn
G  Warehouse or factory building
X  Worker's housing
Y  Worker's housing

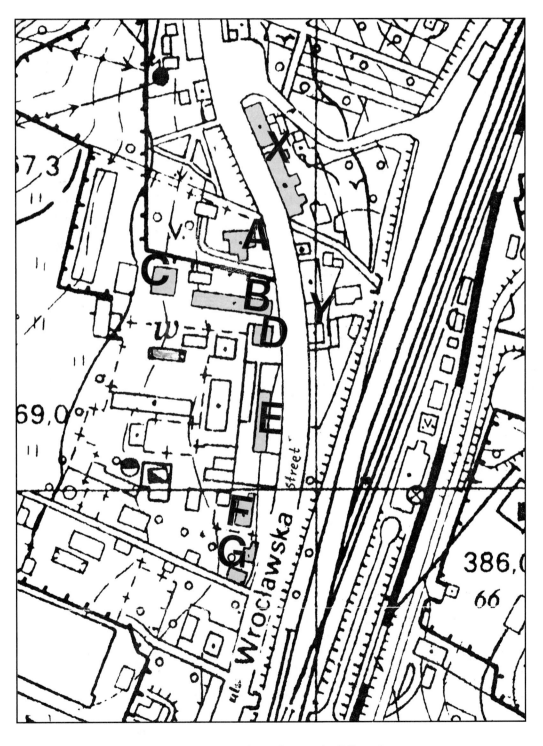

Map with location of Ohme factory buildings in 1994.

Photograph of the Ohme factory offices in Waldenburg in **1923**.

Photographs of the Ohme factory building site today. View from western edge of Pelcznica valley to southeast.

Photograph of the Ohme factory building site in the late **1800s**.

Photographs of the Ohme factory buildings in **1923**.

Photographs of the Ohme factory buildings today, viewed from the northwest.

Photographs of the Ohme factory buildings today, viewed from the southwest.

Photographs of the Ohme factory buildings today, viewed from Wrocławska Street.

Photographs of the Ohme factory glazing room in 1923, first floor of Building B.

Photographs of the Ohme factory glazing room today, first floor of Building B.

Photographs of the Ohme factory painting room in 1923, second floor of Building B.

Photographs of the Ohme factory painting room today, second floor of Building B.

# Materials

The raw materials utilized in the production of Old Ivory China during one month in **1919** is illustrative of the massive quantities required in this manufacture. The Ohme factory imported three wagon loads of **15** tons each of clay from Lohnig, Silesia, an area approximately **30** kilometers north of Nieder-Salzbrunn. At the same time, four wagons of **15** tons each of blue clay were shipped in from Jarischau-Rauske, Silesia, an area **30** kilometers northwest of Nieder-Salzbrunn. The local clays are what give the Old Ivory China its distinctive cream-gray translucent appearance and fine quality.

Two grades of gypsum were imported for production. A lesser grade came from Naumburg (one wagon load per month) which was an area on the Quais River in Silesia approximately **80–100** kilometers northwest of the Ohme factory. The finer grade of gypsum came from the town of Ellrich, near Nordhausen in the Hartz Mountains in West Saxony. This area is over **500** kilometers northwest of the town of Nieder-Salzbrunn. Another fine grade of gypsum came from Krolpa, Thuringa, which was approximately **400** kilometers northwest of the factory.

Kaolin was also a difficult commodity. Though the area of Silesia was rich in kaolins, particularly in Kalno, around **20** kilometers northwest of the factory, Saarau which was **25** kilometers northwest, Jarschau-Rauske which was **30** kilometers northwest, and Ruppersdorf which was **100** kilometers to the northeast. Unfortunately, all of these deposits of kaolin were heavily tainted with iron deposits, making them unacceptable for use in fine porcelain manufacture.

Instead the Ohme factory had to import the kaolin from two locations. The best sources of kaolin were from Sodau and Chodau, near Karlsbad, Bohemia, which was **250** kilometers southwest of the factory, and Kemmlitz, near Mugelin and Ochatz, Saxony, which is almost **500** kilometers northwest of the Ohme manufactory (near Leipzig).

Quartz sands were mined locally in Grussau, Silesia. Chalk had to be imported from Stettin in Pomerania, and feldspar from Wunsiedel, near the German-Bohemian border.

The hard coal to fire the furnaces and kilns came locally from the Waldenburg and Altwasser underground mines. Likewise, the gas to power the remaining kilns came locally from the August Richter Gas-Works (after **1906**).

# Decoration

Over the years, the Porcelain Manufactory Hermann Ohme employed several designers and artists to hand paint the borders of the Old Ivory China and to hand decorate the various decals utilized in production. Some of the early designers included:

Paul von Hampel (born **1874** in Ohlau, Silesia). From **1903**, he was the professor of book art and graphic art at the State School in Silesia.

Hugo Scheinert (born in Zabkowice Slaskie, Silesia). He was the instructor for the drawing classes at the first level of the King Art and Handicraft School.

Erich Erler-Samaden (**1870 – 1946**). He was the brother of Fritz Erler and was apprenticed to Albrecht Baers.

In **1906**, the factory listed three additional principal designers: Erich Kleinhempel, Reinhold Vetter (whose monogram RV is found on many pieces), Amanda Vetter (whose monogram AV is almost as prolific).

It is interesting to note that porcelain decoration was one of the few areas of art that was readily open to women of that era.

The designs represented on the porcelains of Old Ivory came, in part from the works of Catherine Klein. She was born in Berlin, Germany, in **1861**. She received her art education from the schools of Munich and Berlin. From the late **1880s** to the early **1900s** her designs appeared on many porcelains. Most certainly, the Waldenburg Decalcalomania Factory utilized her designs in their decals.

It is clear from the following examples that the Klein watercolors are the inspiration if not the design for many of the Ohme Old Ivory patterns. Of particular note are the soft pink center roses of **#82** taken directly from the Klein print which forms the last plate of the series.

The decals were applied to the clear glazed blanks. The china painters then applied the ivory colored matte background. The pieces were then taken to the designers who hand painted white highlights on the decals. They also hand lined the brown outlines of the border patterns (note that on certain patterns, this outlining was done in gold).

Catherine Klein

The Porcelain Factory Hermann Ohme participated in several large exhibitions.

The first of which was a local Silesian exhibition in **1885**. The second was in London in **1891**, in which they received an Honorary Diploma in Class I. In **1904**, they participated in two exhibitions. The first was at Breslauat which they received a gold medal. They then exhibited at the **1904** World's Fair in St. Louis, Missouri. Three more exhibitions are listed for the Ohme factory: **1911** in Posen, **1912** in Sweidnitz, **1913** in Breslau. The Ohme factory even participated in an exhibition during World War I in **1916**, though the location is unclear.

Though it was obviously necessary to advertise a product, to date, there have been no brochures or newspaper articles or advertisements for the Old Ivory or Hotelware lines of Ohme Porcelains. This unfortunate condition will hopefully be remedied as more collectors become aware of the Ohme Porcelain Manufactory and can scour the paper memorabilia of the turn of the century.

Few advertisements can be found throughout Europe for the Ohme factory as their chief export destination was the United States. The following two articles in German publications in **1923** and **1925** respectively do illustrate, however, the importance of the porcelain manufactory to the region.

The Porcelain Factory Hermann Ohme participated in several large exhibitions: 55

The first of which was a local Silesian exhibition in 1885.
The second was in London in 1891, in which they received an Honorary Diploma in Class I.
In 1904, they participated in two exhibitions:
   The first was at Breslau. At that exhibition, they received a gold medal.
   They then exhibited at the 1904 World's Fair in St. Louis, Missouri.

Das Einfamilienhaus des Kunstgewerbevereins für Breslau und die Provinz Schlesien auf der Ausstellung für Handwerk und Kunstgewerbe in Breslau

1904

Porzellan von H. Ohme, Niedersalzbrunn

Berlin 1905. Verlag von Ernst Wasmuth, A.-G.
Markgrafenstrasse 35

Teil-Ansicht der Porzellanfabrik Herm. Ohme, Niedersalzbrunn

# Qualitätstüchtige Produktionsstätte in der Porzellanindustrie

Die deutsche Porzellanindustrie wußte sich in den letzten Jahrzehnten mit nachhaltiger Kraft und Hingabe und mit unanfechtbarer Berechtigung „einen Platz an der Sonne" zu verschaffen. Weit über Deutschlands Grenze hinaus, ja in allen Kulturländern vermochte sie deutschem Können und Wirken achtungsgebietenden und zugleich lohnenden Erfolg zu sichern. Dieser Erfolg ist nicht etwa nur Ausfluß und Folgeerscheinung einer durch mancherlei Umstände bedingten günstigen Konjunktur, sondern das ausgesprochene Merkmal einer in der Ware selbst liegenden Anerkennung. Auch in anderen Ländern wird gutes, in Form und Dekor charakteristisches Porzellan erzeugt, doch kann sich gegenwärtig das deutsche Porzellan allen Auslandsmarken würdig zur Seite stellen. Mit vollem Recht können wir heute von „deutschem" Porzellan reden, von einem Porzellan, das in der Gediegenheit seines Stoffes, in der Natürlichkeit seiner Form und in der Mannigfaltigkeit und Schönheit seiner Ausstattung unübertroffen dasteht.

Zu den Porzellanfabriken, die sich mit Jahren bemüht haben, Mustergültiges, Eigen- und Einzigartiges zu leisten, gehört auch das Unternehmen Hermann Ohme in Niedersalzbrunn in Schlesien. Im Waldenburger Kreis, nahe an der böhmischen Grenze liegend, weist Niedersalzbrunn in Verbindung mit dem umliegenden Bezirk den besonderen Vorzug auf, die zur Herstellung, speziell zum Brennen des Porzellans geeignete Kohle und andere Materialien in ausreichendem Maße zu besitzen. Diesem Umstand ist es vornehmlich zu-

zuschreiben, daß sich in genanntem Kreis in nächster Nähe des bekannten Badeortes Salzbrunn, große, mit allen technischen Neuerungen ausgestattete Porzellanfabriken entwickelten, die -- gleich den Industrien in Bayern, Sachsen und Thüringen — an Porzellanprodukten Tonangebendes zu bieten vermögen. Auch das Ohmesche Unternehmen sieht seit über 40 Jahren darin seine ausschließliche Aufgabe, Porzellan vom einfachsten bis elegantesten Genre in den verschiedensten Stilarten, Stärken und Größen herzustellen. Neben einfachem und mittlerem Gebrauchsgeschirr finden wir unübertroffen durchgebildete Kunst- und Luxusporzellane vertreten. Jedes Jahr gelangt eine beträchtliche Anzahl neuer Formen und Originalmodelle auf den Markt. Techniker, Maler und Modelleure suchen in gemeinsamem Schaffen praktisch Brauchbares und künstlerisch Wertvolles zu bieten. Tassen, Teller, Dessert- und Obstservice, Speise-, Kaffee- und Teeservice, sie alle verraten reifen Geschmack, dokumentieren eine ausgezeichnete Einfühlung in den Charakter des Porzellans und weisen sehr oft faszinierenden Ideenreichtum auf. Neben weißen und dekorierten Porzellanen werden als Spezialität dünne, transparente, in ihrer Feinheit eine hohe technische Kultur voraussetzende Geschirre in Sèvres-Art hergestellt. Was Wunder, daß die Musterzimmer der Fabrik als Ausschau zahlreicher Kostbarkeiten längst ein besonderer Anziehungspunkt einheimischer und ausländischer Einkäufer geworden sind! — Nicht unerwähnt bleibe bei der Gelegenheit, daß das Ohmesche Werk das erste in Deutschland war, das bei der Herstellung des Porzellans den

Malerei, Innenansicht

Verputzstube

Konturdruck verfeinerte und den Buntdruck ein-
führte. Wie sehr die Firma speziell der Ausstattung des Porzellans ihre Aufmerksamkeit
schenkt, das geht besonders daraus hervor, daß
sie in der Malerei zahlreiche erste Kräfte beschäftigt.

Durchschreiten wir die in den einzelnen Abteilungen durchaus modern eingerichtete Fabrik,
sehen wir die vorzüglich geschulte Arbeiterschar
ihre verschiedenen Obliegenheiten verrichten,
dann wird uns der noch mit jedem Jahr ge-
stiegene Umsatz verständlich. Aus ursprünglich
zwei Brennöfen sind mit der Zeit acht, aus
wenigen Arbeitskräften einige hundert geworden.
Heute sind alle Weltteile Abnehmer der Ohmeschen Erzeugnisse.

Ein Unternehmen mit derartiger Leistung
und Produktionsfähigkeit setzt einen starken,
schöpferischen Willen aus dem Grunde voraus,
weil mit Kapital und Arbeitskräften allein ein
stetes Wachstum nicht zu erzielen ist. Dieser
schöpferische Wille verkörpert sich auf das glück-
lichste in dem Begründer Hermann Ohme, über
dessen Entwicklung einige Angaben von Inter-
esse sein dürften. Durch eine mehrjährige Lehr-
zeit in Leipzig und dem späteren Besuch der
dortigen Handelsschule wurde bei Ohme eine ge-
diegene Grundlage für die spätere Wirksamkeit
gelegt. Andererseits wurde bei ihm das innere
Wachstum dadurch gefördert, daß es in den Ent-
wicklungsjahren mancherlei Mühseligkeiten zu
überwinden galt. 1866 sehen wir Ohme als
preußischen Freiwilligen auf den böhmisch-
mährisch-ungarischen Schlachtfeldern, 1870/71
als Offizier des 72. Preußischen Infanterie-Regi-
ments bei den strapaziösen Kämpfen um Metz
und Dijon. Nach den Kriegen etablierte er sich
in Hamburg und wußte aus der jungen Firma
schon nach kurzer Zeit ein blühendes und hoch-
geachtetes Unternehmen zu gestalten. Nach
seiner Verheiratung siedelte Ohme (1875) nach
Waldenburg über und begann dort 1881 am damaligen Bahnhof Sorgau — dem jetzigen Nieder-

salzbrunn — den Bau einer neuen Porzellanfabrik, die 1882 eröffnet wurde. Nach Plänen
des damaligen Technikers, des späteren Teil-
habers der Firma, Herrn E. M. Bauer, unter
Ohmes Oberaufsicht auf Grund neuester Er-
fahrung ausgeführt, bildete dieser Bau Merkmal
und Kennzeichnung einer an geschäftlichen Er-
folgen reichen Periode. Durch die sich häufen-
den Auftragserteilungen mußten mit den Jahren
innerhalb der einzelnen Abteilungen zahlreiche
Umgestaltungen und Erweiterungen vor-
genommen werden. Die rastlose Tätigkeit
Ohmes fand erst mit dessen Tode ihren Abschluß.
Die Firma löste sich nun als offene Handels-
gesellschaft dergestalt auf, daß auch der Teilhaber, Herr E. M. Bauer, zurücktrat. Heute
wird das Werk im Sinne des Gründers von dessen
Erben unter Oberleitung von Hermann Ohme
junior fortgeführt.

*

Als ein in der Entwicklungsgeschichte der
Firma bedeutungsvolles Moment sei auch die
Tatsache verbucht, daß gleich nach der Grün-
dung von Hermann Ohme senior auf einem benachbarten Terrain eine Steinkohlengasanstalt
gebaut wurde. Leider müssen wir es uns an
dieser Stelle versagen, auf den interessanten
Entwicklungsgang des Ohmeschen Werkes näher
einzugehen, doch dürfte schon aus vorliegen-
den kurzen Angaben Wert und Bedeutung des
Unternehmens jedem sichtlich geworden sein.
Aus kleinen Anfängen geboren, wußte sich die
Firma sehr bald weite Kreise tributär zu
machen. Was sie in Geschirr-, in Kunst- und
Luxus-Porzellanen zu bieten vermag, davon gab
noch jüngst die Ausstellung auf der Jahresschau
Deutscher Arbeit in Dresden sprechenden und
überlegenen Beweis. Bei den einzelnen Motiven
sinngemäße kompositorische Gestaltung zu erzielen, mit Wirtschafts- auch Kunstwillen zu
verbinden, mit dem Schmuck auch die Form in
Einklang zu bringen — das ist's, was alle
Ohmeschen Erzeugnisse auszeichnet!

Beamtenhaus

Villa von Herm. Ohme

Die 1881 begonnene und 1882 eröffnete

# Porzellanfabrik von Hermann Ohme
## in Niedersalzbrunn in Schlesien

beschäftigt zur Zeit ca. 350 Arbeiter, für deren Wohl in jeder möglichen Hinsicht gesorgt wird. So unterhält die Firma ein Mädchenheim, welches bis zu 30 auswärtige, unverheiratete oder verwitwete Arbeiterinnen aufnimmt und sorgt durch eigene Badeanlagen auch in hygienischer Beziehung vorbildlich für den Gesundheitszustand der Arbeiter. Der Wohnungsnot trat das Unternehmen ebenfalls entgegen. Durch die Initiative und unter der geistigen Leitung des Ohmeschen Werkes wurde die Baugenossenschaft Niedersalzbrunn gegründet, die trotz der schwierigen Verhältnisse bisher 32 Familienwohnungen in acht Häusern, sowie ein Sechsfamilienhaus herstellte. Jeder Wohnung ist eine der Größe entsprechende Gartenparzelle beigegeben. Außerdem hat die Firma ihren Arbeitern gegen eine geringe Anerkennungsgebühr etwa 7 Morgen Ackerland zur beliebigen Verfügung gestellt.

Wird so in jeder Weise für die Arbeiterschaft gesorgt, verlangt das Unternehmen andererseits auch kräftige Mitarbeit jedes einzelnen Arbeiters und Angestellten. Diese Zusammenarbeit hat bisher die schönsten Früchte gezeitigt.

Einer der acht Öfen dient ständig der Herstellung des beliebten und bekannten Kobaltgeschirres, die während des Krieges aufgegeben, nun wieder in vollem Umfange betrieben wird. Außerdem hat das Haus Ohme das Verdienst, den keramischen Buntdruck eingeführt und den Konturdruck verfeinert zu haben. Die Fabrikation des Werkes beschränkt sich auf künstlerisches Gebrauchsporzellan, insbesondere Tafel- und Kaffeegeschirr von der einfachsten bis zur kostbarsten Ausführung.

Der Gründer der Fabrik, Hermann Ohme senior, der als Leipziger Kaufmannslehrling seine Laufbahn begonnen hatte und ein Mitkämpfer der deutschen Einigungskriege war, starb 1921. Nach seinem Tode schied Herr Bauer, der 17 Jahre hindurch Teilhaber des Unternehmens gewesen war, aus, so daß die Fabrik nebst der benachbarten ebenfalls von Herrn Ohme gegründeten Gasanstalt alleiniger Besitz der Ohmeschen Erben ist. Der Betrieb untersteht jetzt vollständig Herrn Hermann Ohme junior, dem Sohne des Verstorbenen, unter dessen Leitung sich die Werke weiterhin aufsteigend entwickeln. Da die Ohme-Werke zum großen Teil für den Export arbeiten und in der gesamten Kulturwelt, besonders aber in den Vereinigten Staaten ihre Abnehmer finden, ist ihr weiteres Gedeihen auch in wirtschaftlich kultureller Hinsicht zu begrüßen.

# Competitors

The chief export destination of Old Ivory Porcelains and Hotelware was the United States of America. From all research available, America was the only export destination.

In the year **1919**, for example, the Porcelain Manufactory Hermann Ohme exported per month: one wagon load of gypsum molds, four wagon loads of pottery (Hotelware), and three wagon loads of luxury porcelains (Old Ivory). This figure is better understood for its grand scale when it is realized that each wagon load represented **15** tons. Therefore, for instance, **45** tons of Old Ivory China was exported per month in **1919**. This figure would suggest that **540** tons of Old Ivory was sent to America in **1919** (plus **720** tons of Hotelware).

If we even consider this amount from **1881** to **1928**, over **20,000** tons of Old Ivory China was sent to our shores over the years of factory operation. The figure is staggering. Obviously, the market for china of this sort was large and profitable. It is no wonder that competition was brisk.

At this time, there were **21** porcelain manufactories in the same region of Silesia as the Porcelain Manufactory Hermann Ohme. Many of them produced china remarkably similar to Old Ivory. Some even utilized the same name to identify their china. For collectors of Old Ivory today, this can cause tremendous confusion in identification of those pieces of Old Ivory China which were actually produced in the Ohme factory. In addition, there was the G. Schultz factory of Painting in Freiwaldau, and a faiance in Bunzlau.

The largest and most influential of the competing local manufactories were C. Tielsch Company A.G., in Altwasser, Waldenburg, Silesia. This appears to be the largest of the manufactories in Silesia. In **1915**, at the height of production, the company utilized **12** round kilns, two tunnel-kiln systems, and **28** other kilns. At that time, the factory employed about **1,500** employees. Even at the beginning of the recession of **1928**, the factory boasted **1,250** employees.

Krister A.G., in Waldenburg, Silesia. In **1928**, the factory utilized **14** round kilns and had **1,097** employees. Note that several of the small factories produced only earthenware, technical porcelains, or pottery.

Listed below are the **21** manufacturers located in Silesia. In addition are the locations of the G. Schultz Painting Factory, the Waldenburg Decalcomania Manufactory, and the Bunzlau Faiance.

Please note that the numbers preceding each entry refers to the locations on the map of Silesia which follows.

| | | | |
|---|---|---|---|
| 1. | H. Ohme | (1881 – 1928) | Nieder-Salzbrunn |
| 2. | F. Prause | (1884 – 1936) | Nieder-Salzbrunn |
| 3. | C. Tielsch | (1845 – 1945) | Altwasser, Waldenburg |
| 4. | C. Krister | (1831 – 1926) | Waldenburg |
| 5. | J. Schachtel | (1859 – 1945) | Charlottenbrun |
| 6. | A. Rappsilber | (1860 – 1928) | Konigszelt |
| 7. | C. Walter | (1873 – 1933) | Striegau/Stanowitz |
| 8. | G. Pohl | (1869 – 1932) | Schmiedeburg |
| 10. | K. Steinmann | (1868 – 1931) | Tiefenfurt |
| 10. | R. Reinhold | (1872 – 1931) | Tiefenfurt |
| 10. | E. Leber | (1914 – 1933) | Tiefenfurt |
| 10. | C. Tuppack | (1916 – 1935) | Tiefenfurt |
| 10. | P. Donath | (1890 – 1916) | Tiefenfurt |
| 11. | R. Britze | (1824 – ?) | Freiwaldau |
| 11. | G. Herkner | (1836 – ?) | Freiwaldau |
| 11. | H. Schmidt | (1894 – 1923) | Freiwaldau |
| 11. | R. Tietz | (1929 – 1945) | Freiwaldau |

| | | | | |
|---|---|---|---|---|
| 13. | R. Teichmann | (1888 – ?) | Sorau |
| 14. | R. Schlegelmilch | (1869 – 1938) | Tillowitz |
| 14. | E. Schlegelmilch | (1852 – 1938) | Tillowitz |
| 15. | P. Giesel | (1877 – 1915) | Breslau |

Additional factories:

4.   Waldenburg Decalcomania Manufactory
9.   Bunzlau Faiance
12.  G. Schmidt Factory of Painting

From 1896, all 14 major factories utilized decals and designs of the Waldenburg Declacomania Manufactory. Then in 1900, the factories came together to form the Union of German Porcelain Manufactories.

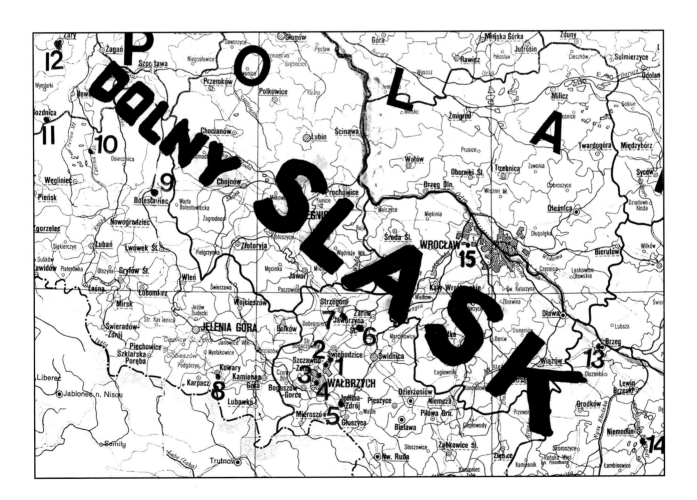

Map of Silesia with locations of the 21 porcelain manufactories.

# The Porcelains

## Marks

The concrete dating of the marks on Ohme porcelains is a subject of controversy. Depending on the resource text on marks used, dating of the individual marks is extremely variable. In fact, there are more than just discrepencies, there are absolute contradictions depending upon which author is consulted. Rather than providing actual time scales for the marks, it must suffice at this time to arrange them into a rough chronology. Actual dating of the individual marks will have to be left to future research where possible.

Each porcelain factory had a mark to identify its porcelain products. Factories used a variety of marks over the years of operation, often revolving around a central theme. The theme represented some aspect of the porcelains, the manufacturer, or merely a whim of the owners. The theme of a mark may be abandoned by future managers or owners of the factory. Thus, there can be a substantial accumulation of marks attributable to one particular factory, especially if it remained in operation for many years.

The marks of the Porcelain Manufactory of Hermann Ohme revolved around only one central theme during the majority of its operation. The basic factory mark on all porcelains of the Ohme factory was an inverted fleur-de-lis surmounted by a circle punctuated at each side with small diamonds. When viewed, this combined mark symbolizes an "O" and an "H" representing the initials for Ohme, Hermann. Above this mark is a

stylized crown. Below this mark on some pieces is the country of origin printed in block capital letters in an upright arc. The three countries of origin are Silesia, Prussia, and Germany.

The earliest marks are short and thick. The later marks are elongated and thinner, at first large, then smaller. Still later marks have a double outline. These marks appeared in four colors: dark blue, light blue, green, and brown. In addition, the country of origin may be in an orange-brown.

The choice of country of origin mark aids in the chronology to some extent. The names Silesia and Prussia will only be present on the china before **1918**, when Germany became the Deutsches Reich. Silesia was utilized for the entire period of **1882 – 1918**, however, Prussia was only utilized from approximately **1902 – 1918**. Germany was used throughout the period of production (**1882 – 1928** or later), so its presence is of little consequence in the determination of a time scale.

Additional factory marks also help to arrange chronology. The earliest marks were a large, thin "X" with or without a tiny stylized crown centered below the crossing. This mark always appeared with the original factory mark. Note that the only pieces located with the "X" without a crown were the portrait pieces.

The next mark was a plain horizontal oval replacing the fleur-de-lis and circle. Within the oval was the word SAXE in capital letters. A small six-pointed star was centered below the oval and the stylized crown was centered above. The use of the word SAXE was probably to connote some relation to Meissen porcelains manufactured in the Saxony region, a term synonymous with quality. This mark appeared alone or in conjunction with the original factory mark. The inclusion of this mark on a particular porcelain piece does not appear to have any significance or value.

The next two marks were shield shaped. An hour-glass outline surrounds the complete original factory mark. Above the hour-glass is a scroll containing the name OHME in capital letters. This combined mark is then surmounted by a small diamond. A corresponding diamond is centered at the bottom of the hour-glass portion. The word "Silesia" may be below in block capital letters in an upright arc.

This mark came in two forms, large and small, both in red and green, and always accompanied by the original factory mark. There is no indication which of these marks predates the other. Just as in the previous case with the SAXE mark, the inclusion of these shield marks on a piece does not seem to hold any significance. Indeed, the marks have been found on both Old Ivory and Hotelware line pieces alike.

A still later mark was actually a variation of the original factory mark. The upright arc which was the area for the country of origin is replaced with an OHME in curvilinear capital letters. The country of origin is absent or is relocated above in an inverted arc. The mark was in light blue and was utilized from 1918 to 1924.

The final factory mark came during the reorganization after Hermann Ohme Sr.'s death in 1921. The mark consisted of a large bulbous crown. Below the crown was the word Ohme in script in an upright arc, highlighted below by a thin curved line. Below this line was the word Germany in block capital letters in a slight upright curve. The mark was in light blue. It was utilized only after 1922.

The next categories of marks were those designating Old Ivory. The marks were always in capital block letters in reddish-brown. The left side may be outlined by several different filigrees. Pattern numbers may be present to the right or below. The oldest known mark in this category is the "Old Jvory" mark. In German, "J" is synonymous with "I." The

appearance of the "J" on this mark dates them as the first mark, probably pre-dating the #4 pattern which is usually marked with an "I."

The blanks were named, often in French, the notable exception being Worcester. There was a preponderence of blank names beginning with the letters A, C, and E. These marks did not appear on all pieces. Many blanks have never been identified by an official name, and were simply left without title. The marks could be in block, capitals, or script. Each blank name always appears in the same way, however. The color was most often dark blue, but may also be the reddish-brown.

The pattern marks were numbers. The earliest numbers were Roman numerals. The later patterns were numbered in Arabic. Not all pieces were numbered. Cups were almost never numbered and creamers were rarely. Many numbers were hand altered to represent a different pattern (not having the stamp for that particular number, a frequently used number was substituted and then altered). Later numbers may be entirely hand written, making differentiation from artists numbers difficult.

Artists numbers were smaller and always hand written. All pieces had either artist number or initial, or both. Some of the artists whose initials or numbers appear on Old Ivory are listed in the "Designer" section later in the book.

The remaining miscellaneous marks fall into three categories. The first category is comprised of specialty pattern names, such as Kilarney Rose, Pamela, Perruche, Orion, or Les Inseparables. For reasons known only to the Ohme factory management, and for the first time, names rather than numbers were used to identify a pattern.

The second category were the import marks, such as dedose, depose, or a variety of symbols. And the third category are the unidentified marks of unknown significance.

In addition to the multitude of marks utilized by the Porcelain Manufactory Hermann Ohme, several competitor factories whose backstamps either resemble Ohme marks or utilize the name Old Ivory for their product are listed on the next page. Their inclusion here is solely for purposes of clarity.

*These examples must not be confused with the products of the Porcelain Manufactory Hermann Ohme.* Though temporally related, and originating in the same region or near the vicinity of the Ohme factory, they are, none-the-less, totally distinct lines of china. The individual company lines will be more fully presented in the section entitled "Competitors" later in the book.

Of special note is the first mark. It is so similar to the mark used by Ohme as to be confusing. Add to that the fact that Tielsch produced a line of Old Ivory China. Imagine the confusion if a piece of porcelain containing that mark and the Old Ivory backstamp were to surface. Fortunately, this situation has not occurred.

The authors wish to express their sincere appreciation to Carl and Jenna Kuttruff for their diligent and exacting research on the marks of the Ohme factory. Through their efforts the compilation of this chapter was greatly facilitated.

## NON-OHME COMPARISON MARKS

C. Tielsch (C.T.) Altwasser, Silesia, 1895
Note the similar fleur-de-lis to Ohme. This company did market Old Ivory.

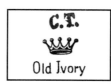

C. Tielsch (C.T.) Altwasser, Silesia, 1875 – 1935
This line of Old Ivory, though well-detailed did *not* come from the Ohme porcelain factory.

Bloch & Co. Eichwald, Germany 1882 – 1930
Note the similarity to the Saxe mark of Ohme. To the consumer, Meissen was synonymous with quality.

Three Crown China Altenburg, Germany, 1881 – 1953
Note that this Old Ivory mark is *not Ohme*. Designs are similar to Old Ivory line of Ohme.

Eagle China Altenburg, Thuringer, Germany, 1881 – 1953
The only pieces found are the Thistle pattern which bear absolutely *no resemblance* to Ohme Old Ivory.

Strigauer factory Stanowitz, Germany, 1873 – 1927
The La Touraine line of Old Ivory, though well-detailed bears *no resemblance* to Ohme products.

Strigauer factory Stanowitz, Germany, 1873 – 1927
St. Pm line of Old Ivory, though well-detailed, *did not* come from the Ohme porcelain factory.

K. Steinmann & Co. Tiefenfurth, Silesia, 1868 – 1938
Though prolific, the quality and design of this line does not approach the workmanship of the Ohme wares.

Tettau Porcelain Factory Tettau, Bavaria, 1916
Royal Bayreuth is a well-known and respected china. However, its Old Ivory bears *no resemblance* to Ohme.

Unknown company Germany, date unknown
Though interesting in style and design, again, these pieces bear *no resemblance* to the Ohme line.

## ALL KNOWN OHME FACTORY MARKS

Ohme Factory mark **1883 – 1892** Inverted small and squat fleur-de-lis mark with stylized crown & "O" above. Mark is in dark blue. No printing above or below.

Ohme Factory mark **1892 – 1902** Inverted long fleur-de-lis mark with stylized crown & "O" above. Mark is in blue. No printing above or below.

Ohme Factory mark **1892 – 1902** Inverted long fleur-de-lis mark with stylized crown & "O" above. Mark is in green. No printing above or below.

Ohme Factory mark **1892 – 1902** Inverted long fleur-de-lis mark with stylized crown & "O" above. Mark is in brown. No printing above or below.

Ohme Factory mark **1888 – 1902** Inverted small and squat fleur-de-lis mark with stylized crown & "O" above. Mark is in dark blue. Dark blue Silesia below.

Ohme Factory mark **1892 – 1918** Inverted large and long fleur-de-lis mark with stylized crown & "O" above. Mark is in blue. Blue Silesia below.

*The Porcelains – Marks*

Ohme Factory mark **1892 – 1918**
Inverted large and long fleur-de-lis mark with stylized crown & "O" above. Mark is in green. Green Silesia below.

Ohme Factory mark **1892 – 1918**
Inverted large and long fleur-de-lis mark with stylized crown & "O" above. Mark is in brown. Brown Silesia below.

Ohme Factory mark **1912 – 1918**
Inverted large and long fleur-de-lis mark with stylized crown & "O" above. Mark is in orange. Note later blue mark on same piece.

Ohme Factory mark **1912 – 1918**
Inverted large and long outlined fleur-de-lis mark with stylized crown & "O" above. Mark is in blue. Blue Silesia below.

Ohme Factory mark **1916 – 1918**
Inverted large and squat outlined fleur-de-lis mark with stylized crown & "O" above. Mark is in blue. Blue Silesia below.

Ohme Factory mark **1892 – 1921**
Inverted large and long outlined fleur-de-lis mark with stylized crown & "O" above. Mark is in blue. Blue Germany below.

Ohme Factory mark **1892 – 1921**
Inverted large and long fleur-de-lis mark with stylized crown & "O" above. Mark is in green. Green Germany below.

Ohme Factory mark **1892 – 1921**
Inverted large and long fleur-de-lis mark with stylized crown & "O" above. Mark is in brown. Brown Germany below.

Ohme Factory mark **1892 – 1912**
Inverted large and long outlined fleur-de-lis mark with stylized crown & "O" above. Mark is in blue. Brown Germany below.

Ohme Factory mark **1892 – 1912**
Inverted large and long fleur-de-lis mark with stylized crown & "O" above. Mark is in green. Brown Germany below.

Ohme Factory mark **1908 – 1918**
Inverted large and long fleur-de-lis mark with stylized crown & "O" above. Mark is in blue. Blue Prussia below.

Ohme Factory mark **1908 – 1918**
Inverted large and long outlined fleur-de-lis mark with stylized crown & "O" above. Mark is in green. Green Prussia below.

**34**

*The Porcelains — Marks*

Ohme Factory mark **1908 – 1918**
Inverted large and long fleur-de-lis mark with stylized crown & "O" above. Mark is in brown. Brown Prussia below.

Ohme Factory mark **1918 – 1919**
Inverted large and long fleur-de-lis mark with stylized crown & "O" above. Mark is in blue. Brown Germany at bottom.

Ohme Factory mark **1919 – 1920**
Inverted large and long fleur-de-lis mark with stylized crown & "O" above. Mark is in blue. Script made in Germany in brown below.

Ohme Factory mark **1918 – 1922**
Inverted large and long outlined fleur-de-lis mark with stylized crown & "O" above. Mark is in blue. Printed Germany in Blue above. Curvilinear block OHME in blue below.

Ohme Factory mark **1918 – 1922**
Inverted large and long outlined fleur-de-lis mark with stylized crown & "O" above. Mark is in blue. Curvilinear block OHME in blue below. Blue Germany at bottom.

Ohme Factory mark **1922 – 1928**
Round stylized crown mark. Mark is in blue. Written Ohme with curved line in blue below. Printed blue Germany following same curve at bottom.

Ohme Factory mark **1892 – 1902**
Printed SAXE in an oval topped by a stylized crown. A small five-pointed star centered below oval. Entire mark is in brown.

Ohme Factory mark **1892 – 1912**
Small green factory mark in the long style encased in a red outlined shield. Green Ohme printed across the top of shield which is topped by a diamond. Green Silesia below. Note older mark beside on same piece.

Ohme Factory mark **1912 – 1918**
Small green factory mark in the outlined style encased in a red outlined shield. Green Ohme printed across the top of shield which is topped by three feathers. Green Silesia below. Note newer mark beside on same piece.

## OLD IVORY MARKS

Old Ivory Mark
Old Jvory (old German spelling of J instead of I) with filigree #1. Pattern number in Roman numerals at the end.

Old Ivory Mark
Old Ivory with filigree #1.

Old Ivory Mark
Old Ivory with filigree #1. Pattern number in Roman numerals at the end.

Old Ivory Mark
Old Ivory with filigree #1. Pattern number in Roman numerals below.

Old Ivory Mark
Old Ivory with filigree #2. Pattern number in Roman numerals below.

Old Ivory Mark
Old Ivory with no filigree.

Old Ivory Mark
Old Ivory with no filigree. Pattern number in Roman numerals below.

Old Ivory Mark
Old Ivory with no filigree. Pattern number in Arabic numerals below.

Old Ivory Mark
Old Ivory handwritten. Hand-written pattern number in Arabic numerals below.

**Blanks Marks**

Blanks Marks
Etoile blank with filigree #3.

Blanks Marks
Mignon blank with no filigree.

Blanks Marks
Elysee blank with no filigree.

Blanks Marks
Eglantine blank with no filigree.

Blanks Marks
Clairon blank with no filigree.

Blanks Marks
Worcester blank with filigree #1.

Blanks Marks
Carmen blank with no filigree.

Blanks Marks
Louis XVI blank with no filigree.

Blanks Marks
Rivoli blank with no filigree.

Blanks Marks
Alice blank with no filigree.

Blanks Marks
Multiple blanks of the vases. Some are marked by a pattern name or grouping. The most popular is Les Inseparables (a boy and girl in Eduardian costume). Other names are Orion, Carmen etc.

Blanks Marks
Though more appropriately a pattern mark (patterns are numbered, not named), these named patterns are mentioned here. Note that some also include a number (eg.: III) Other names are Killarny Rose, Pamela, etc.

**37**

**Pattern Marks**

**Pattern Marks**
Mark in Roman numerals.

**Pattern Marks**
Mark in Arabic numerals.

**Pattern Marks**
Mark in Roman numerals. Mark hand changed at factory from X (ten) to XX (twenty).

**Pattern Marks**
Mark in Arabic numerals. Mark hand changed at factory from 201 to 204.

**Pattern Marks**
Mark in Roman numerals. Mark hand written at factory (34). Note artist mark below in Arabic numerals. Here, it is evident the difficulty in deciding if the hand-written mark is the pattern number or artist mark.

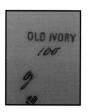

**Pattern Marks**
Mark in Arabic numerals. Mark hand written at factory (100). Note artist marks below which are less clear and ordered.

**Miscellaneous Marks**
Artist mark — initials, number, or both. Hand written and small. This number is often confused as a pattern number.

**Miscellaneous Marks**
Gold Ivory denoting a particular line of china. The patterns are the same as Old Ivory, however the background is a matte golden yellow tone with stamped gold borders.

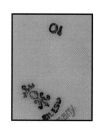

**Miscellaneous Marks**
Gold "10" — a stamped gold number. Unknown significance. Numbers from 7 to 12 and 35 have been found, however, the number 10 is the most common. A gold "M" also found.

**Miscellaneous Marks**
An oval bearing the words "Maison T. Dimier – Geneve." Mark is in brown. Note the older factory mark as well as the SAXE mark. Mark is in French meaning the house (or store) of T. Dimier of Geneva.

**Miscellaneous Marks**
The "X" is, thus far, found only on the vases. Mark is in black or brown. Its significance is unknown. Note that this vase is marked Inseparables, not the usual *Les* Inseparables.

**Miscellaneous Marks**
Depose. Meaning registered for export. Found only on later pieces. The French phrasing may indicate New Orleans as destination. Note the brown "Made in Germany" with the script "depose" in place of Silesia.

**Miscellaneous Marks**
Five petaled flower or star. Mark is in dark blue. Of unknown significance.

**Miscellaneous Marks**
"Mstr." in gold. As this is on a mustard pot, it may represent mustard, or it may designate a master line, or something else entirely.

**Miscellaneous Marks**
Gloriosa with FEU DE FOUR. Feu de four means kiln fired. The French phrasing may indicate New Orleans as port of import. Note the depose in block letters rather than script.

**Miscellaneous Marks**
Cicle containing the block letters "IN." Mark is in black. Unknown significance.

**Miscellaneous Marks**
A double ring outline fenestrated at the top with a stylized crown and containing the block-printed CELEBRATE around the bottom. A light blue OHME fleur-de-lis is centered. CLUNY in block below circle.

**Miscellaneous Marks**
Here, a factory decorator has truly left his or her mark. Actually an original fingerprint of the decorator from the gold firing permanently preseved in the china.

# *Blanks*

To this date there are **20** separate identified blanks or china styles in the Ohme porcelains. A blank refers to the shape of plates, bowls, cups, and pots. The Old Ivory decoration has been found on **18** of the **20** blanks.

In addition, there are **31** unidentified blanks. Single pieces have been found in each of these styles, mostly cups and saucers. Further research may reveal an entire line of china, but for purposes of this book, they are merely noted as individual, unidentified blanks. The other notable exceptions are the vases. It is felt that these shapes represent individual examples specifically manufactured as vases only and do not represent a line of dinnerware.

It is important to understand that Ohme placed the same pattern on several different blanks. This variety of shapes has caused tremendous confusion among collectors. For example: #16 pattern on the typical Clairon blank looks very different than on the Carmen or "Empire" blank.

In some cases, utilizing the same pattern decal on a different blank assigned a new number to the pattern. For instance: the #16 pattern decal on the Clairon blank is #16; however, the #16 pattern decal on the "Florette" blank is #57. Likewise, the #8 pattern decal on the Clairon blank is #8, but, on the "Florette" blank is #44.

If this had been the consistent numbering scheme, there would be little or no confusion. However, the Ohme factory often placed the same pattern decal on different blanks and then identified them with the same pattern number. The most notorious is #16. This pattern decal has appeared on almost every blank shape and is almost always identified with a backstamp that reads #16. One can easily imagine the confusion which ensues when various shapes of cups, bowls, and serving pieces appear with the same number and decal. Identification becomes a nightmare.

For purposes of clarity, it must be remembered that the china is identified by the blank name rather than the pattern number. This is the most difficult habit to break when identifying Old Ivory China. Collectors are used to referring to pieces as a #16, and not a Clairon blank with the #16 pattern. Unfortunately, there is no other way to provide an accurate description of a piece of Old Ivory than to provide the blank name first.

This diversity of shape has prompted collectors to find alternate names for the same piece. Nowhere is this confusion better illustrated than with the waste bowl. When presented with #16 on the Clairon, Eglantine, Carmen, and Alice waste bowls, the collectors were forced to be creative.

Thus, one became a waste bowl, the second an oyster bowl, the third a finger bowl, and the fourth a rose bowl. In reality they are all waste bowls, but, merely in different blank styles of Ohme. This situation also means that the Alice waste bowl does not necessarily go with the Clairon dinner set even though it has the same #16 pattern.

Blanks are identified in the Ohme factory by names. The names were stamped on the backs of some of the pieces. Names such as Clairon, Eglantine, and Elysee have become well known to the collectors of Old Ivory. The names are usually in French, with the notable exception being Worcester.

The meanings and choices of names are obscure. For instance, the name Clairon is the French word for a trumpet call. However, it may as easily represent a proper name. Ohme often used women's names to identify a particular blank (eg. Alice). Clairon may have been created for the stage name of the then famous French stage actress Claire Joseph Hippolyte Leris de la Tude (1723 – 1803). Obviously an unwieldy name for the stage, she shortened it to Clairon.

Unnamed blanks, for purposes of identification, have been assigned names by the authors. The names reflect the shape and design of the individual blank and have been kept in the traditional French flavor. These blank names appear in quotations to differentiate them from the documented blank names.

The ten documented blank names are

Clairon
Eglantine
Elysee
Etoile
Carmen
Alice
Mignon
Rivoli
Louis XVI
Worcester

Those ten blanks assigned names are

"Empire"
"Florette"
"Deco"
"Deco Variant"
"Alice Variant"
"Nouveau"
"Triomphe"
"Quadrille"
"Acanthus"
"Panier"

The blanks have been arranged roughly in order of availability. The most common examples first. The least represented blanks last.

There is a rough chronology to the blanks. This chronology is subject to debate and there is no corroborative evidence beyond the particular Old Ivory patterns which appear on each blank.

The earliest blanks appear to be Etoile, Mignon, Elysee, Clairon, and Eglantine.

"Empire," "Florette," Carmen, "Nouveau," Worcester, and Louis XVI make up the second wave.

The later blank patterns seem to be Alice, Rivoli, "Deco," "Triomphe," "Panier," "Quadrille," and "Acanthus."

### CLAIRION

### EGLANTINE

### ELYSEE

## "EMPIRE" aka STANDARD, FLUTED

## CARMEN

## "FLORETTE" aka FANCY, FLOWERED

## "DECO" aka 200 BLANK

### ALICE

### MIGNON

## *LOUIS XVI*

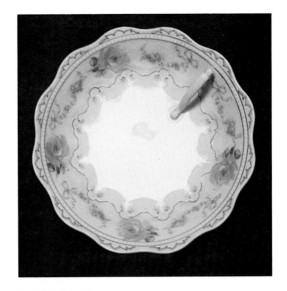

## *RIVOLI aka HEXAGON*

## *ETOILE aka JVORY*

## "NOUVEAU"

## WORCESTER

## "DECO VARIANT"

## "ALICE VARIANT"

## "TRIOMPHE"

## "QUADRILLE"

## "ACANTHUS"

## "PANIER"

## "SWIRL"

# *Unidentified Blanks*

Please also note that not all of the identified blanks have documented examples of Old Ivory. A few of the blank lines have only been identified in the clear glazed Hotelware.

The preceding have been the only identified blank lines (those which contain multiple pieces that have been cataloged) This list does not complete the full spectrum of Old Ivory from the Porcelain Manufactory Hermann Ohme.

The following photographs illustrate the unidentified blanks. Most of the blanks located have been cups. It is possible that an unidentified cup may match another unidentified blank line (or named blank) already listed. Should this situation arise, the numbering of the unidentified blanks would be altered. However, this alteration would be in the form of elimination of a number rather than reorganization. This elimination would create a blank space in the numbering sequence, but, the other entries would remain constant for identification purposes.

#B1

#B2

#B3

#B4

#B5

#B6

#B7

#B8

#B9

#B10

#B11

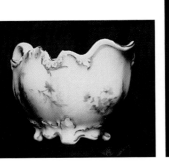

#B12

#B13

#B14

#B15

#B16

#B17

#B18

#B19

#B20

#B21

#B22

#B23

#B24

#B25

#B26

#B27

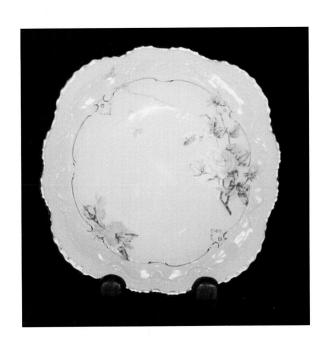

#B28

#B30

#B29

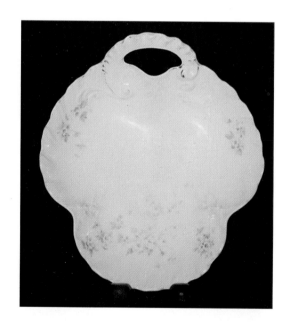

#B31

Oyster plate. Similar to Carmen and Worcester. No mark. Unknown if this is indeed an Ohme Factory Product.

# Filigree

The term filigree refers to the decorative gold banding on the china. In the case of Old Ivory China, the banding is usually a circle separating the clear-glazed center of a plate or bowl with the ivory colored matte rim. In a few instances, the gold band was utilized instead as the border of the pieces. This situation must not be confused with the hand painting of the embossed border pattern on some patterns (notably #32). The filigree is a decal, applied before firing as a single unit, or it is a gold stamp to produce a repetitive pattern on the edge.

The type of filigree used varied from pattern number to pattern number, but was always consistent within a pattern number (with the exception of factory errors). The identification of the gold filigree is essential in the matching of unnumbered pieces to existing known pattern numbers. Often, the only difference between two pattern numbers is the gold filigree used.

For example
#16 differs from #84 only by filigree
#17 differs from #22 only by filigree
Perhaps the best example is a group of pattern numbers: #25, #30, #34, and #40 all have the identical pattern decal. If one had an unnumbered piece, there would be a choice of four possibilities for a match.

The first step is to check for the blank used (see previous section). #25 and #30 are on the Clairon blank. #34 and #40 are on the "Empire" blank.

This differentiation still leaves a choice of two in each case. The difference is in the filigree. It is interesting to note that #25 and #34 share the same filigree as do #30 and #40. It becomes clear that all pieces of information are needed to make a positive identification.

But, what if the piece does not have a filigree, such as a cup and saucer. In this case it would be impossible to make an exact match. It does not matter, because such a piece without filigree would fit into either pattern number without detection.

The following is a listing of all known filigree patterns. The filigrees have been identified by a letter of the alphabet. In the Pattern section of this book, the appropriate letter is placed in the identification box with each corresponding pattern number.

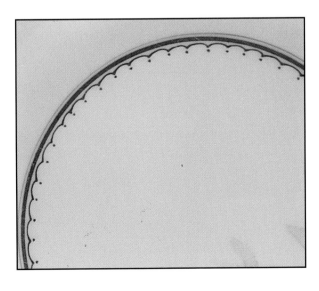

A

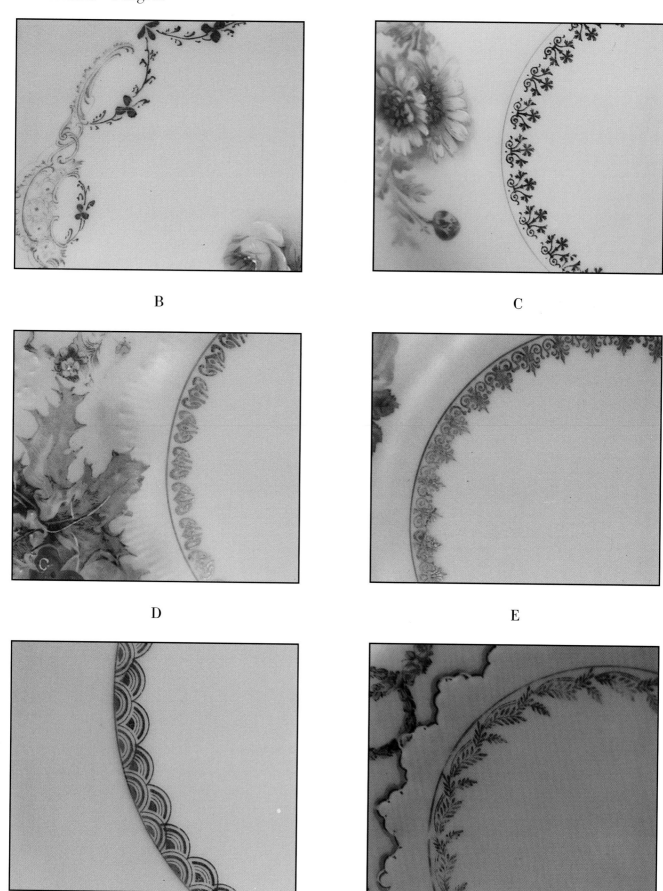

B

C

D

E

F

G

H

I

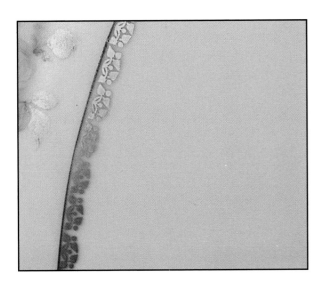

J

K

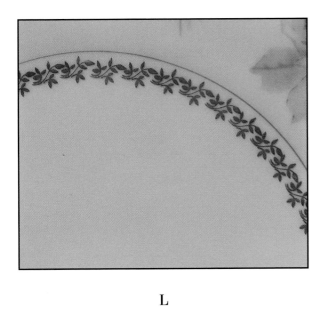

L

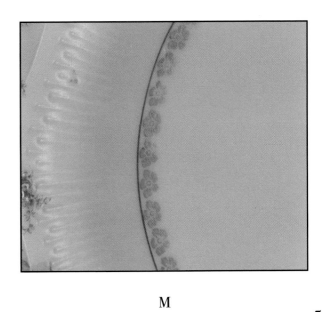

M

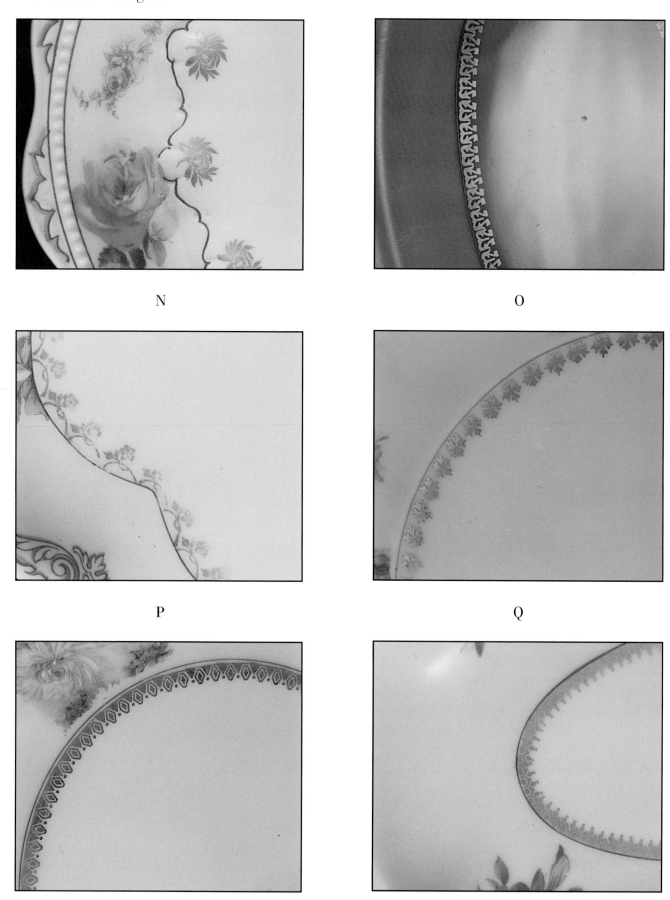

N

O

P

Q

R

S

T

U

V

W

X

Y

Z

AA

BB

CC

# *Patterns*

The patterns of Old Ivory China form the bedrock for the identification of individual pieces. The patterns refer to the decoration of the china. It denotes the decal used (both the main decal and the accessory decals), the filigree applied, the color of the border decoration, and the style of blank utilized. Once again, it is vital to note that the pattern number in no way refers to the shape of the china. The shape is denoted by the blank, which is named and not numbered.

The patterns of Old Ivory China are sequentially numbered (with a probable gap before the #200 series) and are arranged in chronological order. To date, the earliest pattern number identified is #4 and the last pattern number found is #204. In between, there are many gaps, including the large one before #200. It is unclear how far into the numbering after #160 the Ohme Factory went before jumping to the #200 series.

The earlier gaps represent pieces which have not as yet been identified with two possible exceptions. Both exceptions appear early in the numbering system. It must be reiterated that these are only possibilities. In the future, pieces bearing these numbers may be found.

The first exception may be the numbers 1, 2, and 3. By the use of the backstamp Old Jvory, which is the older style of labeling in Germany, it seems logical to assume that the pattern of yellow roses with rust shading on the Etoile blank (identified in this book as #U16), may represent one of the pattern numbers 1, 2, or 3. As there has never been a piece of #U16 found with a pattern number, perhaps the earliest china did not have the backstamped number at all, but, rather, was identified in a catalog only. Only later, with the advent of #4 did the china possess the written backstamp. This theory is only conjecture, and there is no evidence to corroborate or refute it.

The second exception is a tad more concrete. It is well known that in Europe, during the period that Old Ivory China was produced, the number 13 was considered unlucky. So much so, that many European buildings do not have a 13th floor. It seems reasonable to presume that the Ohme factory may not have produced a pattern #13. Again, conjecture, but with a slightly more concrete base of assumption.

Most of the patterns of Old Ivory were flowers. Few exceptions exist. Of note are the holly berries of #17, #22, #39, #62; the fruits around #99; and, of course, #203. Of the flower decals utilized, by far the most common is the rose, including the open rose and the wild rose. Decals were often repeated in several different patterns, varying only by blank, accessory decal, or filigree to create a separate pattern number.

The earliest pattern numbers were printed in Roman numerals. The numbers were located either after the Old Ivory mark or below it. To refresh our memories of forgotten Latin: I represents 1, V represents 5, X represents 10, L represents 50, and C represents 100. The list goes on, however, by this time the Ohme factory had switched over to Arabic numerals (1, 2, 3, 4, 5, etc.).

Further confusion arises in the use of the Roman numerals for numbering. There could never be more than three of one letter in a row. Therefore, III = 3, but IIII was not used for 4. Instead, the Romans used subtraction. To clarify this concept (I hope), a smaller number placed after a larger number is added to it. Eg.: V = 5; VI = 5+1 = 6. On the other hand, a smaller number placed before a larger number is subtracted. Eg.: V = 5; IV = 5-1 = 4.

The only numbers that can be placed before another number had to begin with a one (I = 1; X = 10; C = 100, etc.). Numbers were only placed before the next highest number category. Eg.: "I" can go before V and X, but not XX, L, or C. Therefore 19 is XIX and not IXX. I could go on boring you with this Latin 101 lesson, but you already have the basics.

In fact, you apparently know more than the Ohme factory workers. China has been found with some interesting convolutions of Roman numeral backstamps. Each was an attempt to change a more frequently used number into a pattern number in shorter supply, but this does not excuse the behavior.

Pattern numbers such as XXVIIII to represent 29

do not exist in Latin numbering. Twenty-nine is written XXIX. The Ohme workers took the ubiquitous backstamp for #28 (XXVIII) and hand added an extra I to denote the less common 29. Ohme workers frequently hand altered backstamps both in Roman numerals and Arabic. Backstamps for #204 were often created by changing the 1 in #201 to a 4.

Unfortunately, quality control was not always diligent and pieces with backstamps which should have been altered, and were not, have slipped through. For example: a #15 pattern backstamp was often created by changing the I in XI (#11) to a V. Sometimes, the alteration was forgotten, and the final piece of #15 bears the mark #11. One can readily see how this would greatly add to the confusion in an already overwhelming morass of numbers, both identified and not.

In addition, the artist number is completely hand written. This would, theoretically pose no problem in identification, as this smaller hand-written number could not be confused with the stamped larger pattern number. Unfortunately, in later years, and on higher pattern numbers, the Ohme factory completely abandoned the printed backstamp on many of its pieces. Thus, the pattern numbers, too, were hand written.

Now, the potential for confusion is evident. If only one piece marked with a hand-written pattern number exists, can we be sure that it is not an unnumbered piece with a slightly larger artist mark (a situation which has occurred with more frequency than is comfortable). In the end, one must throw up their hands and make their best educated guess.

In this light, errors in numbering may exist in this book. They should be a rarity, but they are possible. The authors apologize in advance for any errors in pattern identification. Further, we welcome and solicit opposing evidence of pattern identification. If you disagree with one of the pattern numbers listed in the book (exclusive of those prefaced by the letter "U" which stands for unidentified) feel free to contact us and voice your opinion.

The "U" nomenclature was adopted to provide a mechanism for verbal identification of an unknown piece which would be standard to both parties. As a pattern becomes identified, it is removed from the list of "U" numbered patterns and placed within the numbered patterns in the appropriate sequence. Its "U" number is retired so as not to disrupt the other unidentified pattern numbers.

At this time, we, the authors, make a plea to all collectors of Old Ivory. If you find numbered pieces that have not been identified in this book, please provide us with a color photograph of the piece that bears that number. Verbal or written descriptions are subjective and vary so greatly when describing the same piece as to be tantamount to worthless. In this case, a picture is worth a thousand words. We encourage you to beat the bushes for new unidentified pattern numbers. To date, we have identified only about half of the available numbers. There is much work to be done.

The following is a table created to help a collector identify an unknown piece.

There are four elements essential to the matching of an unknown example of Old Ivory China to a known number:

1. The blank — which can be found in the chapter of the same name in this book.
2. The filigree — which can be found in the chapter of the same name in this book.
3. The major decal — the largest design found on the piece.
4. The accessory decals — the smaller decals, usually near the rim.

The table on page **63** provides the first and third pieces of information, the blank and the major decal. With three of the four pieces of information at your fingertips, final comparisons of the accessory decals of each of the pattern numbers listed in that section of the table will provide a rapid method of identification. We hope that the concept proves helpful to you. In addition, extra categories of peculiarities of certain pattern numbers is included at the end of the table which may help to narrow the search.

## Pattern Number Identification Table

**Major Decal and Pattern Numbers**

Brown roses: 5, 16, 28, 31, 32, 33, 57, 60, 67, 69, 70, 71, 75, 76, 82, 84, 115, 116, 117, 121, 123,134, 200, U4, U5, U27, U30.

White, ivory, or creme roses: 12, 16, 32, 57, 60, 63, 78, 84, 123, 200, U3, U4, U5, U9, U27.

Pink roses: 12,14, 20, 63, 67, 68, 78, 82, 114, U3, U6, U9,U37.

Red, rust, or burgundy roses: 103, 107, 115, 116, 117, 134, 145, 200, U8, U27.

Green roses: 5, 28, 29, 31, 33, 69, 75, 115, 116, 117, U18.

Yellow roses: 71, 90, 91, 113, 121, U6, U10, U17, U18.

Peach roses: 25, 30, 34, 40, U6.

Miniature roses: 12, 14, U12, U37.

Open roses: 6, 8, 41, 44, U35.

Wild roses: 11, 21, U14, U31.

Poppies: 15, 61, 92, 120, 122, 202, U11, U15, U24, U39.

Daisies: 10,132, 137, U20, U28, U38, U40.

Swags, garlands, sprays: 14, 19, 69, 70, 76, 91, 114, U8, U12, I18, U37.

Holly: 17, 22, 39, 62.

**Major Decal and Pattern Numbers**

Pansies, Johnny-jump-ups: 97, U23, U29.

Straw flowers, star flowers: 27, 118, 124.

Fruits, nuts: 99, 100, U7.

Peonies: 7, 64.

Tulips: 73, U13.

Chrysanthemums: 201, 204.

Carnations: 65, U34.

Lime green flowers: U19, U21.

Jade green flowers: 64, U22.

Lavendar flowers: 79, U32.

Azaleas: 4.

Hollyhocks: U16.

Iris: U2.

Fuscia: U1.

Buttercups: U25.

Phlox: U33.

Kelly green flowers: 53.

Lily of the valley: 119.

Apple blossoms: 160 .

Blue bands: 203.

## Odd Borders and Pattern Numbers

Matte center to plates: 20, 41, 44, 57, 61, 62,
(not shiny white)    64, 68, 71, 82, 90, 92,
99, 100, 103, 107,
113, 120, 122, 134,
145, U6, U7, U12,
U13, U14, U15, U17,
U18, U19, U21, U22,
U23, U24, U25, U30,
U31, U33, U34, U35.

Gold border: 32, 33, 44, 62, 64, 69, 71, U12,
U13, U14, U16.

Stamped gold border: U10, U30, U31, U34,
U35, U36.

Green scroll: U5, U9, U26, U27.

White border: 20, 68, 70, 75.

Pearlized: U8, U9, U27.

Beige fill in of scroll: 8.

## Blanks and Pattern Numbers

Empire: 15, 16, 21, 22, 27, 28, 29, 31, 32,
33, 34, 39, 40, 53, 75, 78, 84, 99,
100, 103, 107, 113, 116, 117, 118,
122, 123, 145, U6, U7, U8, U9.

Clairon: 7, 8, 10, 11, 12, 14, 15, 16, 17, 21,
22, 25, 28, 29, 30, 63, 65, 67, 73,
82, 84, 90, 91, 97, 115, 119, 122,
160, U39, U40 .

Florette: 20, 41, 44, 57, 62, 64, 68, 69, 70,
71, 75, U13, U14, U15, U16.

Alice: 60, 120, 121, 122, 134, U30, U31,
U32, U33, U34, U35, U36.

Eglantine: 6, 19, 114, U21, U22, U23, U24,
U25.

Deco: 200, 201, 202, 203, 204, U1, U2, U3,
U4, U5.

Rivoli: 61, 92, 124, 132, 237, U10, U11.

Elysee: 4, 5, U19, U20.

Louis XVI: 76, U37, U38.

Carmen: 16, 84.

Etoile: U17, U18.

Worcester: 28, U12.

?Square: U27, U28.

Mignon: U26.

?Pansy: U29.

The following is a pictorial guide of all known numbers and those assigned temporary pattern numbers by the authors.

The pattern number is located in the upper left corner.

The blank is named on the second line. Where more than one blank is listed, it is because the same pattern was used on several blanks, but retained the same pattern number. Eg.: #16 pattern on Clarion, "Empire," and Carmen blanks.

The major decal (and accessory decals where possible) are listed on the third line.

Any special details, peculiarities, or other comparable patterns are listed on the fourth line.

The filigree type is listed on the fifth line as well as some special notes.

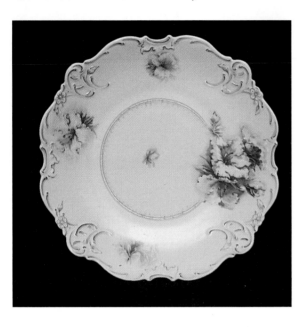

#4
Blank: Elysee
Design: Creme colored azaleas
Gold filigree: A

#5
Blank: Elysee
Design: Brown & green roses
Gold filigree: B

#6
Blank: Eglantine
Design: Brown & green open rose
Note: Same flower as #8
Gold filigree: A

#7
Blank: Clairon
Design: Green & brown peonies
Gold filigree: A

#8
Blank: Clairon
Design: Brown & creme open roses
Note: Tan shaded border flutes
Gold filigree: A

#10
Blank: Clairon
Design: White & yellow daisies, gold center
Gold filigree: C

#11
Blank: Clairon
Design: Brown & green wild roses
Gold filigree: C

#12
Blank: Clairon
Design: Bright pink & creme small roses
Gold filigree: D

#14
Blank: Clairon
Design: Dark pink tiny roses and bows in swags
Gold filigree: D

#15
Blank: Clairon, "Empire"
Design: Pink, aqua & brown poppies
Note: Same design as #120 & #202
Gold filigree: E

#16
Blank: Clairon, "Empire," Carmen
Design: Brown & creme roses
Note: Same design as #84 & #57
Gold filigree: E

#17
Blank: Clairon
Design: Holly berries & teal leaves
Note: Same design as #22 & #39
Gold filigree: F

#19
Blank: Eglantine
Design: Pink, lavender & green garlands
Gold filigree: G

#20
Blank: "Florette"
Design: Pink roses; aqua & lavendar shade
Note: White flowered border
Gold filigree: None; matte center

#21
Blank: Clairon, "Florette," "Empire"
Design: White wild rose; lavender shading
Gold filigree: E

#22
Blank: Clairon, "Empire"
Design: Holly berries & teal leaves
Note: Same design as #17 & #39
Gold filigree: H

**#25**
Blank: Clairon
Design: Peach colored roses
Note: Same design as #30, #34 & #40
Gold filigree: J

**#26**
Blank: "Empire"
Design: Multicolored small straw flowers
Gold filigree: I

**#28**
Blank: Clairon, "Empire," Worcester
Design: Brown & green roses
Gold filigree: H

**#29**
Blank: Clairon, "Empire"
Design: Greenish roses; salmon and
aqua shade
Gold filigree: J

#30
Blank: Clairon
Design: Peach colored roses
Note: Same design as #25, #34 & #40
Gold filigree: I

#31
Blank: "Empire"
Design: Brown & green roses
Note: Same design as #28
Gold filigree: J

#32
Blank: "Empire"
Design: Ivory & brown roses
Note: Gold border decoration
Gold filigree: I

#33
Blank: "Empire"
Design: Brown & green roses; peach shading
Note: Gold border decoration
Gold filigree: K

**#34**
Blank: "Empire"
Design: Peach colored roses
Note: Same design as #25, #30 & #40
Gold filigree: J

**#39**
Blank: "Empire"
Design: Holly berries & teal leaves
Note: Same design as #17 & #22
Gold filigree: H

**#40**
Blank: "Empire"
Design: Peach colored roses
Note: Same design as #25, #30 & #34
Gold filigree: I

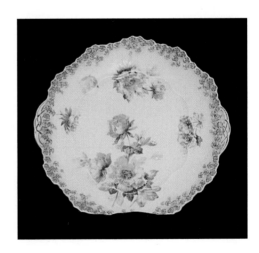

**#41**
Blank: "Florette"
Design: Brown & green open rose; brown border
Note: Same design as #6, #8 & #44
Gold filigree: None

**#44**
Blank: "Florette"
Design: Brown & green open roses; gold border
Note: Same design as #6, #8 & #41
Gold filigree: None

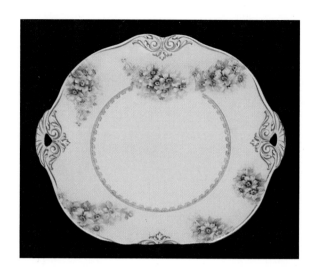

**#53**
Blank: "Empire"
Design: Kelly green small flowers
Gold filigree: I

**#57**
Blank: "Florette"
Design: Brown & creme rose; brown border
Note: Same design as #16, #84
Gold filigree: None

**#60**
Blank: Alice
Design: Creme & brown open roses
Note: Same design as #8 gold border
Gold filigree: I

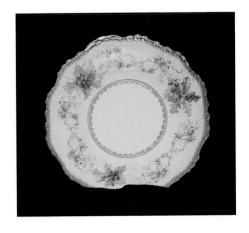

**#61**
Blank: Rivoli
Design: Rust poppies & aqua spray
Note: Same design as #92
Gold filigree: None

**#62**
Blank: "Florette"
Design: Holly berries; teal & brown swags
Note: Gold flowered border
Gold filigree: D

**#63**
Blank: Clairon
Design: Pink & creme roses
Note: Same design as #78
Gold filigree: L

**#64**
Blank: "Florette"
Design: Small green & large brown peonies
Note: Gold flowered border
Gold filigree: None

**#65**
Blank: Clairon
Design: Bright pink carnations
Gold filigree: H

**#67**
Blank: Clairon
Design: Brown roses & pink roses
Note: Combination of #16 & #63
Gold filigree: L

**#68**
Blank: "Florette"
Design: Bright pink baby roses
Note: White flowered border
Gold filigree: None

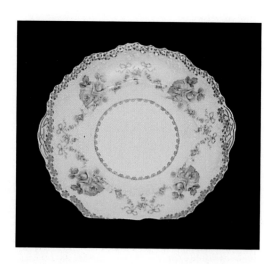

**#69**
Blank: "Florette"
Design: Brown & green roses; swags & bows
Note: Gold flowered border
Gold filigree: I

**#70**
Blank: "Florette"
Design: Brown & green roses; swags & bows
Note: Same design as #69; white border
Gold filigree: M

**#71**
Blank: "Florette"
Design: Small yellow roses & brown roses
Note: Gold flowered border
Gold filigree: None

**#73**
Blank: Clairon, "Empire"
Design: Salmon tulips & aqua spray
Gold filigree: H

**#75**
Blank: "Empire," "Florette"
Design: Brown & green roses
Note: White flowered border
Gold filigree: H

**#76**
Blank: Louis XVI
Design: Brown roses; swags & bows
Gold filigree: N

**#78**
Blank: "Empire"
Design: Pink & creme roses
Note: Same design as **#63**; gold border
Gold filigree: L

**#79**
Blank: "Florette"
Design: Clusters of lavender blooms
Note: Clear center
Gold filigree: None

**#82**
Blank: Clairon, "Empire"
Design: Pink center rose; brown roses at edge
Note: Matte center
Gold filigree: None

#84
Blank: Clairon, "Empire," etc...
Design: Brown & creme roses
Note: Same design as #16
Gold filigree: O

#90
Blank: Clairon
Design: Three yellow roses; smaller roses at edge
Note: Same design as #113; matte center
Gold filigree: None

#91
Blank: Clairon
Design: Three yellow roses; small spray & bow
Note: Same flowers as #113
Gold filigree: ?

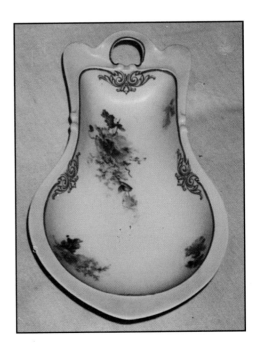

#92
Blank: Rivoli
Design: Rust poppies & aqua spray
Note: Same design as #61
Gold filigree: None

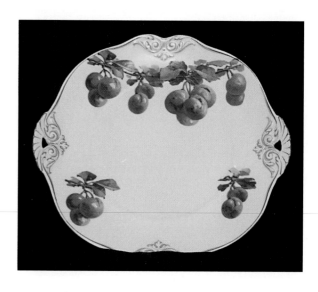

#97
Blank: Clairon
Design: Rust, yellow & purple pansies
Note: May be all purple pansies
Note: Matte center
Gold filigree: None

#99
Blank: "Empire"
Design: Rust-red plums or cherries
Note: Matte center
Gold filigree: None

#100
Blank: Clairon
Design: Rust-colored gooseberries
Note: Matte center
Gold filigree: None

#103
Blank: "Empire"
Design: 3 rust center roses; small flowers at edge
Note: Same design as #107, but offset, matte center
Gold filigree: None

**#107**
Blank: "Empire"
Design: Three rust center roses; smaller roses at edge
Note: Matte center
Gold filigree: None

**#113**
Blank: "Empire"
Design: Three yellow center roses; small brown flowers
Note: Matte center
Gold filigree: None

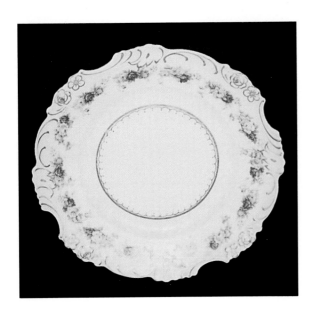

**#114**
Blank: Eglantine
Design: Bright red & pink roses; green leaves
Gold filigree: A

**#115**
Blank: Clairon
Design: Small brown, rust & green roses
Note: Same design as #116 & #117
Gold filigree: I

#116
Blank: "Empire"
Design: Small brown, rust & green roses
Note: Same design as #115 & #117
Gold filigree: J

#117
Blank: "Empire"
Design: Small brown, rust & green roses
Note: Same design as #115 & #116
Gold filigree: H

#118
Blank: "Empire"
Design: Blue, rust, gray & creme star flowers
Gold filigree: C

#119
Blank: Clairon, Rivoli
Design: Yellow & white lily of the valley
Gold filigree: K

#120
Blank: Alice
Design: Pink, aqua & brown poppies
Note: Same design as #15 & #202,
matte center
Gold filigree: None

#121
Blank: Alice
Design: Brown & yellow roses
Gold filigree: P

#122
Blank: Clairon, "Empire," Carmen
Design: Rust-colored large poppies
Note: Matte center
Gold filigree: None

#123
Blank: "Empire"
Design: Brown & white roses
Gold filigree: U

#124
Blank: Rivoli
Design: Brown & creme star flowers
Gold filigree: Q

#132
Blank: Rivoli
Design: White, green & brown daisies
Note: Same as #137
Gold filigree: ?

#134
Blank: Alice
Design: Rusty orange & brown roses
Note: Matte center
Gold filigree: None

#137
Blank: Rivoli
Design: White, green & brown daisies
Note: Same as #132
Gold filigree: R

**#145**
Blank: "Empire"
Design: Rust-colored roses
Note: Matte center
Gold filigree: None

**#160**
Blank: Clairon
Design: Delicate pink & white apple blossoms
Gold filigree: ?

**#200**
Blank: "Deco"
Design: Brown, white & burgundy roses
Gold filigree: S

**#201**
Blank: "Deco"
Design: Orange, pink & purple mums
Note: No center flower; unlike #204
Gold filigree: S

#202
Blank: "Deco"
Design: Pink, aqua & brown poppies
Note: Same design as #15, #120
Gold filigree: S

#203
Blank: "Deco"
Design: Blue band; tan, lavender & black design
Gold filigree: T

#204
Blank: "Deco"
Design: Orange, pink & purple cosmos
Note: Center flowers; unlike #201
Gold filigree: S

#204
Blank: "Deco"
Design: Orange, pink & purple mums
Note: Center flower; alternate
Gold filigree: S

## NO PATTERN NUMBERS

The following is a pictorial reference of the unidentified and unnumbered patterns within the Old Ivory line. The section represents all patterns found to this date by the authors.

For purposes of identification and a standard of description, the patterns are assigned a number beginning with "U." The list is arranged by blank styles (an arbitrary designation) and does not represent chronology. The same decal found on a different blank has been identified as a separate pattern (following the examples of #16 and #57 and others).

Some of these patterns may never have been numbered. Still others may share the numbering of one of the previously identified patterns (as the #16 on Clarion, "Empire," and Carmen).

#U1
Blank: "Deco"
Design: Bright pink fuchsias
Note: Probably # above 204
Gold filigree: V

#U2
Blank: "Deco"
Design: Maroon iris-like flowers
Note: Probably # above 204
Gold filigree: S

#U3
Blank: "Deco"
Design: Soft pink & creme roses
Note: Same design as #U11
Gold filigree: E

#U4
Blank: "Deco"
Design: Brown & creme roses
Note: Same design as #84 – note gold 10
Gold filigree: O

#U5
Blank: "Deco"
Design: Brown & creme open roses
Note: Green border; gold M mark
Gold filigree: AA; pearlized finish

#U6
Blank: "Empire"
Design: Yellow, peach & pink roses
Note: Matte center
Gold filigree: None

#U7
Blank: "Empire"
Design: Brown hazelnuts
Note: Matte center; number around 100
Gold filigree: None

#U8 Killarney Rose
Blank: "Empire"
Design: Red roses with small daisy print
Note: Pearlized finish
Gold filigree: ?

#U9
Blank: "Empire"
Design: Brown, white & burgundy roses
Note: Same design as #200
Gold filigree: E; green border scroll

#U10 Gold Ivory
Blank: Rivoli
Design: Large yellow roses
Note: Leafy gold border
Gold filigree: W (border)

#U11
Blank: Rivoli
Design: Soft pink & creme roses
Note: Same design as #U3
Gold filigree: E

#U12
Blank: Worcester
Design: Pink & yellow Johnny jump-ups
Note: Same deisgn as #U23; gold border
Gold filigree: None; matte center

**#U13**
Blank: "Florette"
Design: Salmon tulips & aqua spray
Note: Same design as #73; gold border
Gold filigree: None; matte center

**#U14**
Blank: "Florette"
Design: White, wild rose-lavender shading
Note: Same design as #21; gold border
Gold filigree: None; matte center

**#U15**
Blank: "Florette"
Design: Pink, aqua & brown poppies
Note: Same design as #15; brown border
Gold filigree: None; matte center

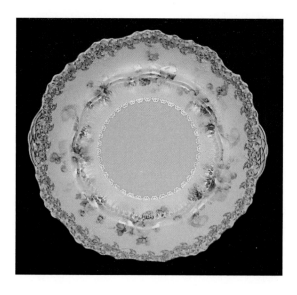

**#U16**
Blank: "Florette"
Design: Multicolored hollyhocks
Note: Gold border
Gold filigree: I

#U17 OLD JVORY
Blank: Etoile
Design: Yellow roses; rust shading
Note: Matte center
Gold filigree: None

#U18
Blank: Etoile
Design: Green roses in a spray
Note: Matte center
Gold filigree: None

#U19
Blank: Elysee
Design: Small lime green flowers
Note: Same design as #U21
Gold filigree: None; matte center

#U20 PAMELA
Blank: Elysee
Design: Daisies on a pale green background
Note: Also in blue background
Gold filigree: A

#U21
Blank: Eglantine
Design: Small lime green flowers
Note: Same design as #U19
Gold filigree: A

#U22
Blank: Eglantine
Design: Small jade flowers; bows & swags
Note: Clear center
Gold filigree: None

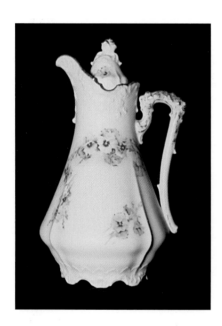

#U23
Blank: Eglantine
Design: Pink & yellow Johnny jump-ups
Note: Gold border
Gold filigree: ?

#U24
Blank: Eglantine
Design: Pink, aqua & brown poppy; rust shade
Note: Same design as #15
Gold filigree: H; matte center

#U25
Blank: Eglantine
Design: White buttercups in spray
Note: Clear center
Gold filigree: None

#U26
Blank: Mignon
Design: Violets with lavender ribbon
Note: Light green trim
Gold filigree: A

#U27
Blank: ? Square
Design: Brown, white & burgundy roses
Note: #200 roses – green scroll border
Gold filigree: ? Pearlized

#U28
Blank: ?Square
Design: Yellow & white daisies
Note: Same design as #137
Gold filigree: ?

#U29
Blank: ?Pansy
Design: Yellow & rust pansies
Gold filigree: ?

#U30
Blank: Alice
Design: Circle of brown (#16) roses
Note: Matte center; gold border
Gold filigree: W or Y (border)

#U31
Blank: Alice
Design: Circle of wild (#11) roses
Note: Matte center; gold border
Gold filigree: W or Y (border)

#U32
Blank: Alice
Design: Pale lavender & pink flowers
Gold filigree: F

#U33 IMPERIAL ALMA
Blank: Alice
Design: Green & lavender shading
Note: Matte center
Gold filigree: None

#U34
Blank: Alice
Design: Hot pink carnations
Note: Matte center; gold border
Gold filigree: None

#U35
Blank: Alice
Design: Pink & white open roses
Note: Matte center
Gold filigree: Z

#U36
Blank: Alice
Design: Three yellow center roses
Note: Same design as #113
Gold filigree: G

**#U37**
Blank: Louis XVI
Design: Pink tiny roses; aqua bows & swags
Gold filigree: ?

**#U38**
Blank: Louis XVI
Design: Small brown & white daisies
Gold filigree: ?

**#U39**
Blank: Clairon
Design: Orange poppies with black centers
Gold filigree: H

**#U40**
Blank: Clairon
Design: White green & brown daisies
Note: Same flower as #137
Gold filigree: ?

## PORTRAIT PIECES

The following is a pictorial reference of the portrait pieces within the Old Ivory line. The portrait pieces of Old Ivory all share a common set of decals. The pictures are of children of a bygone era in various settings or poses. Some of the scenes are named. Eg.: Les Inseparables (the inseparable ones). The portrait decals have been found on vases, pitchers, cups, covered boxes, plates, tea sets, and demitasse sets.

The final two portrait pieces have a different style of decal. These pieces sport a clear glaze and are, therefore, part of the Hotelware line and not traditional Old Ivory.

The last plates in this section are not typical portrait plates. The first is a hunt scene; a popular genre of the time. Though matte glazed and, therefore, potentially of the Old Ivory line, it does not fit well by color or design.

The second example is a fish set which, again fits the category of a gaming piece. Again, the finish is not the traditional Old Ivory, but is in flow blue. The placement of these examples within the portrait pieces is appropriate as many of them also share a non-traditional look for Old Ivory.

**#P1 LES INSEPARABLES**
Type: Vase
Color: Sepia
Design: Boy & girl with guitar

**#P2 ORION**
Type: Vase
Color: Sepia
Design: Boy & girl with flute

**#P3 CARMEN**
Type: Creamer
Color: Green
Design: Boy behind girl facing right

**#P4 UNNAMED**
Type: Plate
Color: Red
Design: Boy behind girl facing left

#P5 UNNAMED
Type: Cup & saucer
Color: Beige
Design: Boy with girl with heads together

#P6 UNNAMED
Type: Vase
Color: Sepia
Design: Boy next to girl facing right

#P78 UNNAMED
Type: Pitcher
Color: Sepia
Design: Boy next to girl facing right (same as #P6)

#P8 LES INSEPARABLES
Type: Cruet?
Color: Sepia
Design: Boy & girl in ¾ length portrait

#P9 UNNAMED
Type: Covered box
Color: Beige
Design: Boy & girl; heads together (same as #P5)

#P10 EROS
Type: Demitasse set
Color: Red
Design: Boy behind girl both directions

#P11 LES INSEPARABLES
Type: Vase
Color: Sepia
Design: Boy & girl with bouquet

#P12 UNNAMED
Type: Vase
Color: Sepia
Design: Boy behind girl facing left

#P13 CLEAR GLAZE
Type: Coffee set
Color: Pastels
Design: Garden scene women & babies

#P15 UNNAMED
Blank: Eglantine
Type: Plate
Design: Pheasant hunt scene; pale green bodrer

#P14 CLEAR GLAZE
Type: Vase
Color: Pale blue
Design: Woman in an empire dress

#P16 UNNAMED
Blank: Eglantine
Type: Fish set
Design: Various species of fish; flow blue border

## SOUVENIR PIECES

The following is a pictorial reference of the souvenir pieces within the Ohme lines. The souvenir pieces are Ohme blanks in either the Old Ivory style or, more frequently, the Hotelware line which have been decorated with historic, commemorative, or commercial decals. This group is a small representation of the many pieces that exist.

Some of the decals were applied at the Ohme factory. Note, the first example on the Mignon blank may have been decorated at the factory. The plate is done in the Old Ivory finish and is replete with the hand-painted border decoration. On all other pieces of Mignon found to date, this matte border region is where the flowered decals appear. If not, then at least an accessory decal would be found. But, the area is void of such decoration. It, therefore must have been intended to be used as a souvenir style piece where such extraneous decoration may distract or detract from the central illustration.

Now, note the second example of the souvenir cup of Otto von Hindenburg. This piece too is assumed to have been decorated at the Ohme factory, however the reason for this assumption is slightly different. This cup was located in the region of the Ohme factory and, therefore, one may presume that it was most likely decorated there.

Other pieces may have been later decorated in the United States. No confirmations can be located at this time. Note the third and fourth pieces. These two pieces belong to the Hotelware line. Examples of these two plates with exactly the same clear glazed designs and decals and without the center illustration have been found. Thus, one may conjecture that the china was purchased as a finished Hotelware piece and the center decal applied later.

The souvenir pieces do, however, often help in dating a particular blank either grossly, by the date applied on the decal, or covertly, by the timing of an event or commemoration or the particular monument or building included in the decal.

#S1
Blank: Mignon
Type: Bowl
Design: State Normal School, Farmington, Maine
Note: Old Ivory; filigree A

#S2
Blank: Unknown
Type: Cup
Design: Otto Von Hindenburg commemorative
Note: Factory designed

#S3
Blank: Alice
Type: Plate
Design: Public school, Leonardville,
Kansas
Note: Clear glazed

#S4
Blank: Triomphe
Type: Plate
Design: Huron College, Huron, South Dakota
Note: Clear glazed

## OTHER DESIGNERS

Occasionally, the Ohme blanks were decorated by one of the eminent design studios outside the Ohme factory itself. Such blank decorating was a common practice at the time, allowing the design studio to concentrate on its artwork while selecting pieces of fine porcelain on which they would be displayed.

The four examples in this section represent such outside design work. The first two examples are designed by the Tatler Studio on an Ohme blank. These designs are freqently encountered on the porcelains of the Royal Schlegelmilch (or R. S.) factories, but can be found on most of the quality china factory pieces of the era.

The clear glazed blank was first china painted with the bold reddish maroon design. The large pictorial decal is applied as a unit to the center of the

plate. Then the gold decoration is applied. The decals are of the Melon Eaters, which is a well known Tatler decoration.

The second two examples are designed and decorated in the Pickard Studios. The clear glazed Ohme blanks are completely hand painted by a single artist who signed the work at the bottom right of the design. The Eglantine creamer and sugar were designed by D. E. Roy and the Alice plate was designed by Challonier.

The flow blue example is not pictured at this juncture as it appears in another section of the book. In addition, it is possible that this flow blue designing was done at the Ohme factory itself. In the interest of clarity and accuracy, its inclusion is elsewhere. A photograph of the fish set is located in the preceding section on Portrait Pieces (#P16).

#D1
Blank: Alice
Type: Plate
Designer: Tatler Studio

The Melon Eaters decal

#D2
Blank: Eglantine
Designer: Pickard Studio
Sugar & Creamer: Red Roses
Artist: D.E. Roy

Blank: Alice
Designer: Pickard Studio
Cake Plate: Strawberries
Artist: Challonier

## COMPANION PIECES

The following is a pictorial reference of the companion pieces to the Old Ivory line. These pieces, though produced by another factory, were apparently designed to go with the corresponding Ohme pieces.

These are factory produced and decorated pieces and should not be confused with hand painted blanks made to look like Old Ivory. These examples will be presented in the hand-painted section of the Hotelware.

Shaving brush

Here, the brush is pictured with the corresponding Ohme shaving mug.

Dresser tray & stickpin holder
Note the raised gold border done in the Nippon moriage style. There is fine detailing on this novel piece.

# *Pieces*

This section concerns the various pieces of Old Ivory which are available within each of the blank styles. Pieces refer to the type of tableware such as plates, bowls, cups, etc. Not all types of pieces existed in each blank style and there is no one blank style which includes every single type of piece. However, some blank lines are more complete than others.

Every attempt was made to locate examples of each and every blank within a specific piece to be represented in the photographic section. Unfortunately, many examples simply cannot be located at this time. Some blank styles had virtually no examples which could be located and photographed.

For collectors, it becomes important to understand the individual availability of a particular blank and pattern, and what pieces have been found within that blank style. For example, a collection of the #16 pattern on the Clairon blank is a reasonably accessible and complete line. To vary the pattern decreases availability. For instance, the #90 pattern on the same blank will be far more difficult to amass a useable set.

To collect an obscure pattern on an unusual or atypical blank is next to impossible. One would have very little hope of collecting a complete china service in the Worcester blank decorated in an Old Ivory pattern. So little of it has been found. Such a collection in the Hotelware is far more accessible. Please bear in mind that nothing is impossible. One of the author's collections is a reasonably complete set of Old Ivory on the Mignon blank. Anything can be accomplished with enough time, patience, diligence, and dumb luck.

Hopefully, the following pages will provide a rough notion of the blank styles which are more complete than others. In this way, collectors can decide for themselves if they wish to collect rare and obscure pieces, or try for a complete table setting.

Most of the pieces which should exist in a porcelain line of the late **1800s** and early **1900s** have been located in Old Ivory or in Hotelware for several of the blanks. Certain pieces are governed by era (eg.: open salts in the early lines and salt shakers in the later lines, etc.). Other pieces, though not located, have been identified as being seen by collectors over the years. They include

Oyster plates — though a possible, unmarked example has surfaced (see last page of Blanks section. Cruets, syrup pitchers, candle sticks.

Commode sets — large pitcher and bowl, toothbrush holder, tumbler, powder jar, and soap dish (or other combination).

This last set raises an interesting question. If a commode set was made in Old Ivory, could there be a chamber pot as well? The prospect evokes such antithetical emotional responses of anticipation and horror. In the end, anticipation wins out and we look forward to the news of such a discovery.

The following is a pictorial guide to the available pieces within each blank style. The arrangement is intended, where possible, to provide consistency in identification. Each example is labled only with the blank style represented.

The items are shown from the most commonly found to the least. In most cases, the same blank styles tend to be the most common, but, to every rule there are many exceptions. Hopefully, this system will be both illustrative and informative.

## PLATES

The plates are flat pieces of china, most often round, truncated, or square. For purposes of Old Ivory, they are always completely symmetric. Measurements are approximations as variations exist between the different blank lines. The importance is not the concrete size, but the relationship of sizes to each other within a particular line.

Plates are found in **15** sizes: eight sizes of indented plates, seven sizes of smooth plates. (Note that two sizes of coupe plates which have not yet been identified but may exist are the small dinner coupe plate at 9½" and the bread coupe plate at 7". The addition of these two examples would raise the number of smooth plates to nine and the total to **17**.)

Indented plates:
    Chargers . . . . . . . . . . . . . . .13"
    Dinner plates . . . . . . . . . . .10"
    Soup plates . . . . . . . . . . . . .9½"
    Small dinner plates . . . . . . .9¼"
    Luncheon plates . . . . . . . . . .8½"
    Salad plates . . . . . . . . . . . .7¾"
    Bread plates . . . . . . . . . . . . .7"
    Dessert plates . . . . . . . . . .6¼"
Smooth plates:
    Open-handled cake plates . . . .11"
    Open-handled cake plates . . .10½"
    Dinner coupe plates . . . . . . .10"
    Luncheon coupe plate . . . . .8½"
    Salad coupe plates . . . . . . .7¾"
    Dessert coupe plate . . . . . . .6¼"
    Butter pats . . . . . . . . . . . .3¼"

Clairon

Eglantine

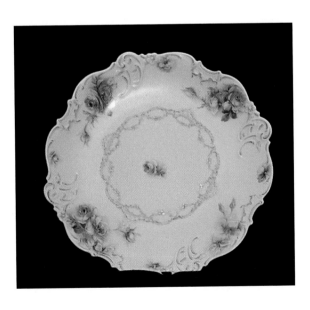

Elysee

"Empire"

Carmen

"Florette"

"Deco"

Alice

Mignon

Louis XVI

Rivoli

Etoile

"Nouveau"

Worcester

"Triomphe"

"Quadrille"

**Cake Plates**

Clairon

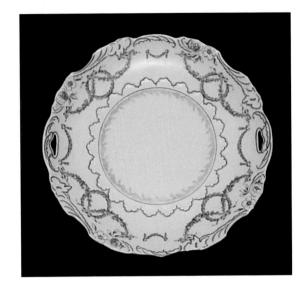

Eglantine

Elysee

"Empire"

Carmen

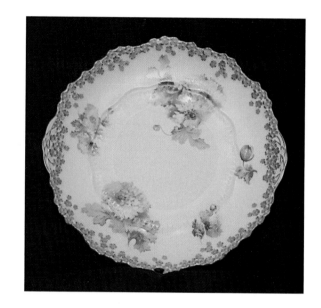

"Florette"

"Deco"

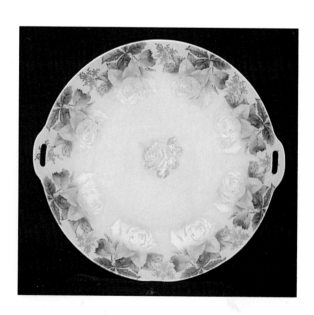

Alice

Rivoli

Louis XVI

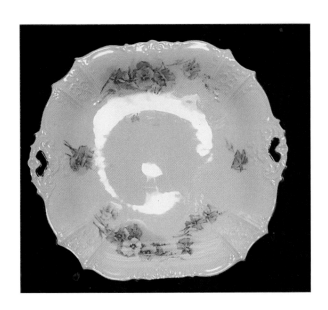

Etoile

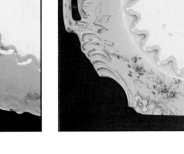

Eglantine
variants #1 & #2

## Butter Pats

Clairon

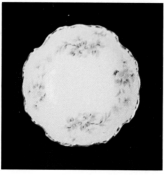

Eglantine

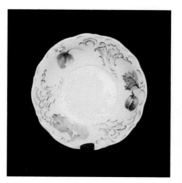

Elysee

"Empire"

Carmen

"Florette"

Mignon

Alice

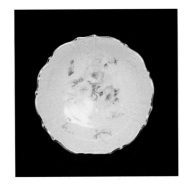

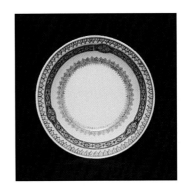

Etoile

"Deco"

Rivoli

Worcester

## PLATTERS

Platters are oblong flat pieces used for serving. They are typically large, and have specified and designated uses by size and shape. The platters are typically oval and have a minute foot encircling the bottom for heat dissipation.

There are six sizes of platters in Old Ivory.

Turkey platter..........**28**″ (and broad)
Fish platter  .........**23**″ (and narrow)
Game platter  ....................**21**″
Large platter  ....................**16½**″
Medium platter ....................**13½**″
Small platter  ....................**11½**″

On the other hand, trays tend to be rectangular with a flat ground bottom. The notable exception is the oval Clairon dresser tray which differs from its platter counterpart by only the flat ground bottom.

There are three sizes of trays in Old Ivory.

Tea tray  .............................21″
Large dresser tray ..................12½″
Small dresser tray ..................11½″

Clairon

Eglantine

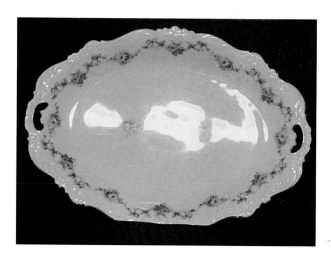

Elysee

"Empire"

Carmen

"Florette"

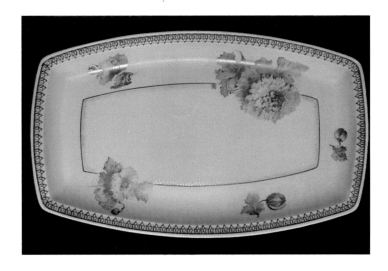

"Deco"

Alice

Mignon

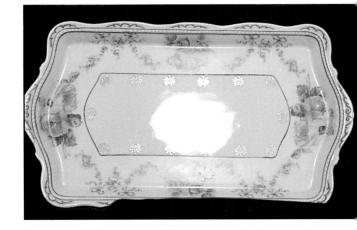

Louis XVI

Rivoli

Worcester

**Fish Sets**

Eglantine fish set
Flow blue style

The Eglantine fish set above contains six small plates, the fish platter, and a sauceboat with attached underplate.

Worcester fish set — clear glazed
The Worcester fish set contains six dinner-sized plates. It is probable that the complete fish set may have been a combination of both.

## ROUND BOWLS

Bowls are round (or square), deep items intended to hold liquids, semi-solids, or multiple small items. The plain bowls are for utilitarian and multiple functions, while the fancy bowls have added elements which make them specific for particular functions and specialized in their design.

The ice cream bowl is an enlarged soup plate. Its low design and large diameter made it functional to hold dollops of ice cream, preventing dripping onto the table, while making it available for spooning.

The nappy is a cereal bowl with an applied handle which begins at the center and radiates to one side. This design permitted lifting the bowl in an elegant manner while not touching one's fingers to the sticky confections contained within.

The footed bowl had a variety of uses, but all centered around the realm of display. The bowl was intended to raise its contents above the other items on the table in order to focus attention on the rarity displayed within.

There are six sizes of plain bowls and three sizes of fancy bowls.

Plain bowls:

Serving bowls ........................10"
Large berry bowls .....................9"
Soup bowls .........................7½"
Cereal bowls.........6½" (and 1" deep)
Oatmeal bowls ......6½" (and 2" deep)
Sauce bowls .........................5½"
Small berry bowls .....................5"

Fancy bowls:

Footed bowls...........................6"
Ice cream bowls ......................10"
Nappys ..............................6½"

Clairon

Elysee

Eglantine

"Empire"

Carmen

"Deco"

Alice

"Florette"

Mignon

Louis XVI

Rivoli

Etoile

Clairon

"Deco"

Elysee

Alice

"Quadrille"

Louis XVI

"Alice Variant"
round center bowl

Top view

"Deco" footed bowl

Top view

"Alice Variant"
footed bowl

Top view

**Serving Bowls**

Elysee
ice cream dish

Eglantine
pierced handled bowl

Clairon
pierced handled bowl

Carmen
closed handled bowl

These pieces are oval or rectangular deep pieces intended for liquid, semi-solid, or multiple small or elongated items. They all have specialized functions. None of these bowls was covered or lidded. In two cases, the bowls came in sets of three which stacked one inside the other for storage. These stackable sets were the bun trays and the three lobed dishes.

There are 17 sizes of oblong bowls.

Oval vegetable bowl ............9½"
Large oval center bowl .........11"
Celery dish ...................11¼"
Pickle dish ...................8½"
Olive dish ....................6½"
Porringer .....................6¼"
Lay down spooner* .............8¼"
Ladle holder ..................6½"
Bun tray ......................12"

Bun tray .........................10"
Bun tray .........................8"
Handled basket ...................8"
Three lobed dish ...............8½"
Three lobed dish ...............7¼"
Three lobed dish ...............6"
Candy dish (bow tie shaped) ....8"
Bone dish (crescent shaped) ..6¾"

*Please note that the lay down spooner, when matched with a small tea cup (3") forms a new set entitled "toast and tea set." The purpose of this set was to provide an oblong deep saucer which could be held at one end by a single deft and adroit finger. This deep stable saucer provided a resting place for a small tea cup and a few small bisquits, kept far from the starched and bleached white gloves the ladies of the era donned for their garden parties and informal brunches.

Clairon

Eglantine

Elysee

"Empire"

Etoile

"Florette"

"Deco"

Alice

Mignon

Rivoli

"Quadrille"

Top view, oval console bowl

**Celery Dishes**

Clairon

Eglantine

Elysee

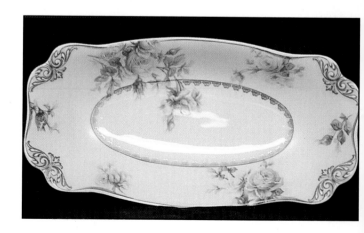

"Empire"

Etoile

"Florette"

"Deco"

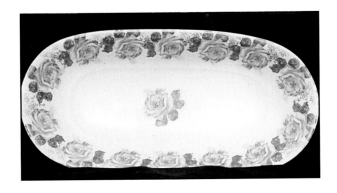

Alice

**Spoon Rests**

"Florette"

Alice

"Deco"

Rivoli

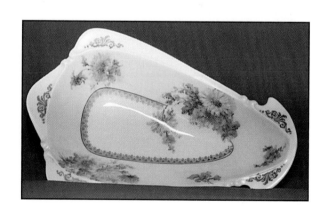

Rivoli

Rivoli

Rivoli toast & tea, "Deco" cup

Rivoli ladle holder

**Shaped Bowls**

"Empire" porringer

"Deco"
3-lobed bowl (3 sizes which stack)

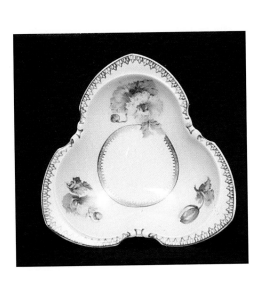

Rivoli 3-lobed bowl

"Alice Variant" scalloped bowl

## Bun Trays

Alice
(3 sizes)

Rivoli

Rivoli

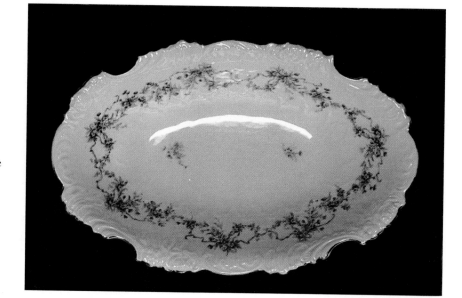

Eglantine

**Baskets**

Elysee

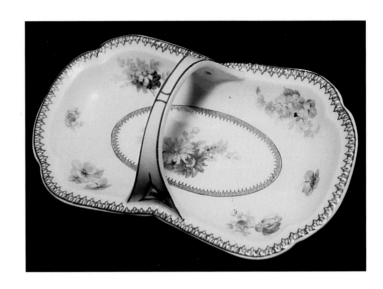

"Deco"

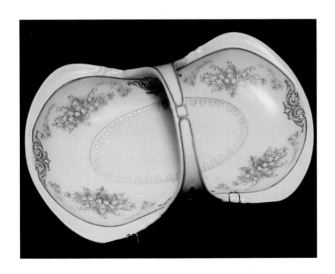

Rivoli

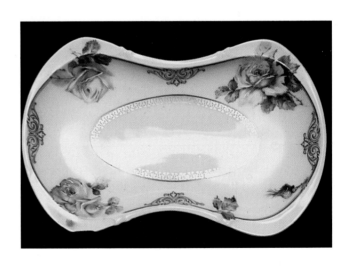

Rivoli
candy dish, bow tie shape

**Serving Bowls**

"Quadrille"
oval center bowl

Top view

Note that the bone dish is found only in one mold, Worcester. Bone dishes, however, have been found decorated in a variety of patterns and designs. The blank is crescent shaped.

## *CUPS*

This section concerns the various sizes, shapes, and uses of the cups. Cups were a very specialized commodity. Each had their specific function which governed their size and shape. For instance, at high tea, which was at three in the afternoon, a large tea cup was served. At five o'clock the smaller tea cup was utilized. The names of the remaining cups clearly indicate form and function.

There are 11 sizes and styles of cups.

Coffee cup & saucer ...........3½"
Tea cup & saucer .............3¼"
5-o'clock tea cup & saucer ......3"
Demitasse cup & saucer........2½"

Chocolate cup & saucer ........2¼"
Bouillon cup & saucer ........3½"
Cider cup & saucer .............3"
Chowder or stew cup.............4"
Moustache cup & saucer ......3½"
Shaving mug ...................3¼"
Egg cup ........................2½"

* Note that the moustache cup is the coffee cup with an internal shield resembling an ice guard. The purpose was to prevent the moustache from touching the liquid in the cup (we who are hirsute of upper lip salute this invention). The cups came in both left- and right-handed versions.

The following photograph is a size and shape comparison of various cup styles.

Bouillon, chocolate, cider, coffee, tea, 5 o'clock tea, demitasse
Clairon blank

**Tea & Coffee Cups**

Clairon

Eglantine

Elysee

"Empire"

**131**

"Alice Variant"

"Florette"

"Deco"

Alice

Mignon

Louis XVI

Etoile

Rivoli

**Chocolate Cups**

Clairon

Eglantine

Elysee

"Empire"

The Porcelains — Pieces

*The Porcelains — Pieces*

Etoile

"Florette"

"Deco"

Alice

"Nouveau"

"Alice Variant"

Rivoli

Rivoli Variant

**Demitasse Cups**

Clairon

Eglantine

Elysee

"Empire"

Carmen

"Florette"

"Deco"

Alice

Mignon

Etoile

Unknown

Unknown

**Bouillon Cups**

Clairon

Eglantine

Elysee

"Alice Variant"

## Moustache Cups

Clairon

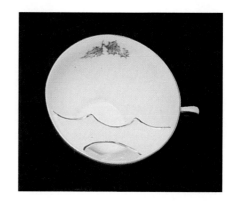

Top view

Eglantine

Top view

Elysee

Top view

"Empire"

Top view

**Shaving Mugs**

Elysee

Top view

Clairon

Top view

**Rare Cups**

Eglantine
egg cup

Eglantine
chowder cup

The egg cup is found in only one blank style (Eglantine). However, there are various pattern decorations.

Only one example of both the chowder cup and cider cup have been found. The chowder cup is in the Eglantine blank and the cider cup is in the Clairon blank.

Clairon
cider cup

## POTS & TEA SETS

The lidded pots have always been a source of confusion in nomenclature for Old Ivory collectors. The variety of shapes and sizes as well as the myriad of spouts has caused great consternation. In light of the multiple blanks produced by the Ohme factory the confusion can be abated. The importance of size in the identification of the function, and thus, name of a pot relies not on its actual measurements, but rather in its size relationship to other pots within its blank line. For purposes of this text, the pots will be discussed individually.

There are four serving pots to a typical Old Ivory dinner set.

The chocolate pot which is the most commonly located and most ubiquitous of the pots. It is large, usually about 9" tall, with a spout that is part of the rim.

The coffee pot which is of approximately equal size to the chocolate pot, and often of similar shape. The spout, however is located further down the side of the pot, separate from the rim. This is one of the rarest pots in Old Ivory.

The teapot which is of shorter stature than the preceding pots, but of wider girth. The spout is located near the bottom of the side of the pot and is usually longer and more curved than its counterparts. Due to variability of size among the different blank styles, there is a great range of heights to the teapots. In some instances, it is actually shorter than the corresponding demitasse pot and in some cases, significantly taller. Few teapots have been located.

The demitasse pot is the smallest serving pot in the Ohme line. It is designed to resemble a miniature version of the coffee pot. Again, the spout originates on the side of the pot, well below the rim. demitasse pots are not rare, but are certainly not plentiful.

The bisquit or cracker jar causes, perhaps, the most confusion in sizing. There are two styles of bisquit jar: tall and short. However, only one style appears in each line of Old Ivory blank. Some of the blanks which use the tall bisquit jar are Clairon, Eglantine, Elysee, Worcester. Some of the blanks which use the short bisquit jar are "Empire," "Deco," Alice, "Triomphe." Comparison of these

styles is evident in the photography section which follows. In addition, there are two sizes of bisquit jars within each Old Ivory line. They are identical in appearance save a subtle side handle change in some lines (eg.: Eglantine).

The sugar and creamer sets come in two sizes. Their style, however, is identical within a given blank. The smaller, or regular sugar and creamer are reasonably common. On the other hand, the larger, or service sugar and creamer are rarities. To further complicate, the "Deco" line has an intermediate size, which may only represent a variation in manufacture as it appears to serve no functional purpose.

The spooner, designed to hold the tea spoons for the tea set is of similar size to the creamer. Rather than having handles, per say, the spooner has decorative knobs or protrusions on each side.

The waste bowl is footed and rimmed to collect the waste (tea egg and leaves) of a tea service. The tall sides prevented spillage and the lip guided the tea egg to its desired destination. The foot was designed to complement the other pieces of the tea set which were all footed. The alternate use as an oyster bowl was facilitated by the barrel shape which held the crushed ice and the wide lip for displaying the delicacies. The bowl is quite wide, but only about as tall as the regular sugar.

The tea tray is a large rectangular tray with a substantial rim and a flat, ground bottom. It is usually 21" in length. It is intended to hold the teapot (or coffee or demitasse), sugar and creamer, spooner, and waste bowl. If there is room, the cups and saucers were also placed on the tray. When used for the chocolate set. The tray housed the chocolate pot, sugar and creamer (the melted chocolate was often unsweetened or bitter chocolate), chocolate cups, and saucers.

The tea tile was intended to insulate the hot serving pots from marring the finish of wooden tables or buffets. The tile is a simple flat ring with a thick rim which extends below the bottom surface to form a thin ring. There is no embossed decoration on the tea tile as this decoration would be counterproductive to its function. The various blank styles were designated by decals of the border decoration applied around the flat upper surface. Few tea tiles have been located.

The toothpick holder is self-explanatory. The smallest of the pots, it is a narrower version of the waste bowl and is usually approximately 2¾" tall.

The jam jar is a lidded, straight sided, cylindrical container for preserves or jellies. The lid is often slotted to accomodate a spoon. In later years, with the advent of condensed milk, a hole was drilled in the bottom of the jar before firing to make a new container: the condensed milk container. The hole was provided in the bottom to be able to push the empty can out from the bottom rather than risking injury by touching the metal rim of the can (remembering the crude can openers of that day). Though condensed milk containers have never been found in Ohme Old Ivory, they have been found in some of the competitors' lines.

The mustard pot, another self-explanatory piece is a small lidded pot with a single handle on the side. Being only 3¾" tall, its shape resembles the sugar bowl (minus one handle). The lid is slotted to hold the specialized mustard spoon (a white small straight ladle).

The previous examples outline the 16 pots and tea set items found in Old Ivory. In the interest of clarity, the following photographs illustrate some size comparisons among the pots. Bear in mind that measurements vary greatly between blanks, but the relationships of the various pots remains constant within a given blank.

Alice
chocolate pot, coffee pot, teapot, demitasse pot

Eglantine
chocolate pot, teapot, demitasse pot

Eglantine
bisquit jar, teapot

"Deco"
teapot, demitasse pot

Eglantine
service sugar bowl, sugar bowl, mustard,
spooner, toothpick, creamer, service creamer

Alice
bisquit jar, service sugar bowl,
sugar bowl

## Chocolate Pots

Clairon

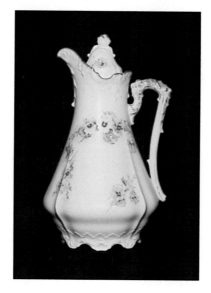

Eglantine

Elysee

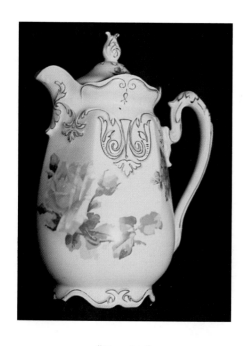

"Empire"

Carmen

"Florette"

Rivoli

"Deco"

Alice

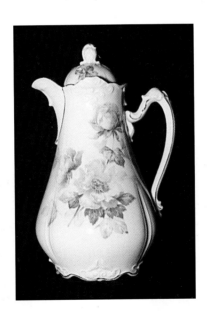

"Noveau"

"Triomphe"

Etoile

**Coffee Pots**

Worcester

"Deco"

Alice

"Deco Variant"

"Panier"

Unknown

Coffee set
creamer, coffee pot, sugar cup

**Teapots**

Eglantine

"Deco"

Alice

"Deco Variant"

**Demitasse Pots**

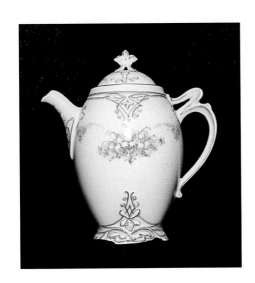

Clairon

Eglantine

Elysee

Carmen

"Florette"

"Empire"

Alice

Mignon

Etoile

"Deco"

**Toothpick Holders**

Clairon　　　Eglantine　　　Elysee　　　"Florette"

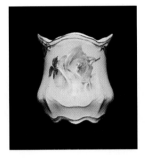 

Carmen　　　"Quadrille"

**Sugar & Creamer**

Clairon　　　Eglantine

Elysee

"Empire"

Carmen

"Florette"

"Deco"

Alice

Louis XVI

Worcester

Rivoli

Mignon

?Square

"Deco Variant"

Unknown

Unknown

**Spooners**

Elysee

Clairon

Eglantine

Carmen

Eglantine Variant

Etoile

Tea set

The typical arrangement is the teapot, sugar, creamer, spooner, waste bowl, and cups and saucers on a platter or tea tray.

## Cracker Jars

Clairon

Eglantine

Elysee

Worcester

"Empire"

"Deco"

Florette

Rivoli

Alice

"Triomphe"

Eglantine Variant

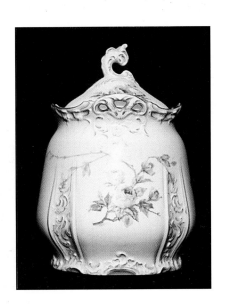

Etoile

## Waste Bowls

Clairon

Eglantine

Alice

Carmen

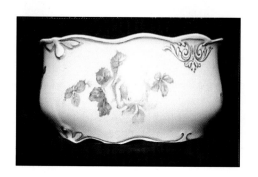

"Quadrille"

Worcester

Mignon

"Alice Variant"

### Jam Jars

No example of a jam jar converted to a condensed milk container has been found in Old Ivory or Hotelware of the Ohme factory. However, such pieces have been located in competitors' lines. The only difference in the condensed milk container is a small finger hole cut in the center of the bottom of the jar. The purpose was to allow one's finger to push up against the bottom of the condensed milk can placed inside the porcelain container and remove the empty can.

Alice

"Deco"

"Deco Variant"

## Mustard Pots

Clairon

Eglantine

Elysee

Etoile

Carmen

Alice

"Deco"

Mignon

**Tea Trays & Tiles**

Alice
tea tray and matching tea set

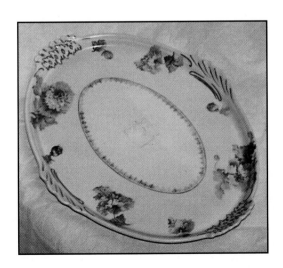

Tea tray, unknown blank, #15 pattern

Tea tile, only one blank (Alice),
various pattern decorations

## *SERVING PIECES*

This section concerns the various serving dishes available in the Ohme lines. Few of these examples are available in all, or even most of the blank styles. The serving dishes are all hard to find pieces, with many of the examples being rare. The pieces are divided into two categories: covered and open.

There are five covered serving dishes and nine open serving dish styles.

Covered serving dishes:
    Covered vegetable (round)........10½"
    Covered vegetable (oval) ..........10½"
    Soup toureen ........................13"
    Covered butter dish (with insert) ..7¼"

    Small covered sauce boat ..........8½"
    Cheese dish........................9¼"
Open serving dishes:
    Gravy boat ........................8½"
    Mayonnaise & underplate ........6½"
    Ramakin & underplate ........4¼"+5"
    Tazza or cake stand ..................9"
    Compote ............................9"
    Open salt (individual) ..............1¾"
    Salt & pepper shakers ...........2¾"
    Muffineer or sugar shaker ...........4"
    Water pitcher .....................8" tall
    Center handle double server ........12"

## Covered Vegetable

Clairon

Carmen

"Deco"

Alice

Mignon

Alice Variant

"Deco Variant"

Worcester

## Soup Toureens

Clairon

Elysee
Coll. Muzeum Okregowego Walbrzych,
nr inw. MWC - Malgorzata Robaszynska
(photo by D. Gdesz)

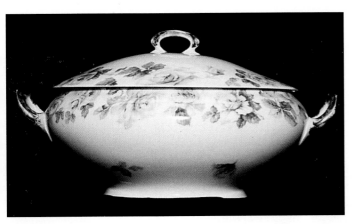

Alice

Alice Variant

"Deco Variant"

"Deco Variant"
top view

Etoile

Swirl

## Covered Butters

Clairon

Carmen

Alice

Mignon

**Butter Insert**

Eglantine

Only one blank has ever been found for the butter dish inserts, regardless of the blank of butter dish in which it was found. It is therefore assumed that the insert only came in one style, that being Eglantine.

**Cheese Dish**

Clairon

The Cheese dish underplate is roughly the size of a dinner plate. Only one example has been found, so it is unclear if an insert was utilized (as this example was without insert). It is assumed that an insert would resemble the butter insert.

**Gravy Boats**

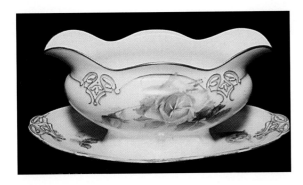

Clairon

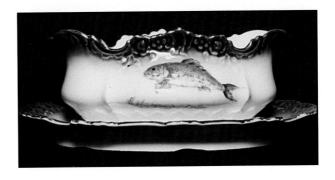

Eglantine

Etoile

Carmen

**167**

Alice

"Alice Variant"

"Deco"

Mignon

**Mayonnaise Dish**

Eglantine
Note that these blanks may be decorated as
Clairon, "Florette," "Empire," Carmen, etc.

"Empire"
Note that these blanks may be decorated as
Clairon, "Florette," "Empire," Carmen, etc.

**Ramakin**

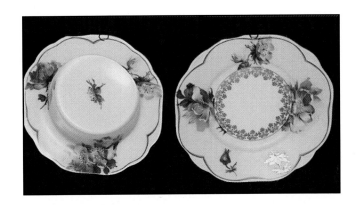

"Quadrille"
with two parts separated

Alice
underplate

Elysee
may not be OHME

**169**

## Compotes/Tazzas

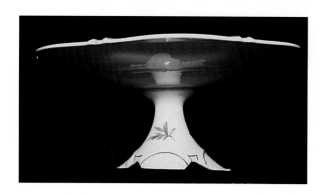

Tazza or cakestand
Rivoli blank

Top view

Compote
Alice blank

Top view

**Salt & Peppers**

All pieces are the same blank (Louis XVI).
Blank names represent decorations only.

Clairon

"Empire"

"Florette"

"Deco"

Louis XVI

Alice

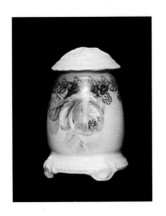

"Florette"

Salt and pepper shakers were a later invention, superceding the traditional salt dips or individual open salts. It is, therefore, unlikely that they will be found in the earlier blank lines. However, it is hoped that other examples will be uncovered.

**Water Pitchers**

All pieces are the same blank ("Acanthus").
Blank names represent decorations only.

"Acanthus"

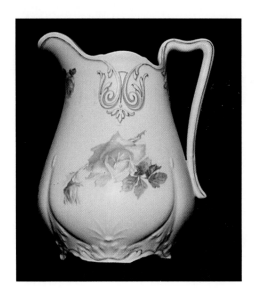

"Empire"
long

"Empire"
short

"Florette"

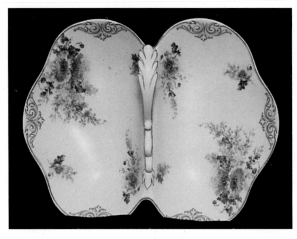

Divided serving piece with center handle
12" x 9½" x 4"

Muffineer, one blank
(Louis XVI). Various
pattern decorations

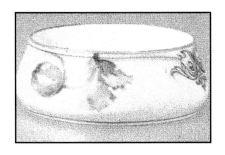

Open salt — Alice blank
Photo by permission of Susan C. Smith
from the *Third Book of Individual Open
Salts.* By Allan B. & Helen B. Smith;
Published by The Country House, Topsham, ME. 1976.

Covered sauce toureen
Eglantine blank

## DRESSER SETS

This section concerns the dresser sets (those porcelain products not utilized at the dinner table). These pieces are rare and difficult to find in sets. It would be in this section that the commode set and the candlesticks would be included if examples are ever located.

One important distinction is between a platter and a tray. Platters are generally oval and have a ring around the bottom to raise the platter off the table. The bottom, therefore, is glazed. On the other hand, the trays tend to be rectangular and have a flat, ground bottom (with the notable excep-

tion of the oval Clairon dresser tray which is indistinguishable from its platter counterpart, save the ground bottom).

There are eight pieces in this section.

Dresser tray ..................... 12½"
Dresser tray ..................... 11½"
Hat pin holder
Powder jar (lidded)
Covered trinket ..................... 3"
Hair receiver
Toothbrush holder ............. 4" tall
Vase ........................... variable

Eglantine
dresser set

"Deco Variant" hair receiver & powder box

Etoile
large trinket box

Etoile
small trinket box

**Vases**

Note that to date only two examples of vases within the actual Old Ivory line have been found which do not contain a portrait.

Hotelware vases without portraits have been located, however.

For purposes of this text, the remaining vases are located in the Portrait Pieces section immediately following.

"Deco Variant"

Unknown

Eglantine toothbrush holder

# *Hotelware*

The Porcelain Manufactory Hermann Ohme produced two distinct lines of china. The first was the Old Ivory line. The second was a line of Hotelware. This series of china was a more moderately priced and more easily produced line.

The same blanks were utilized for both Old Ivory and the Hotelware. Both lines were clear glazed. However, in the case of Old Ivory, the glazed bisque blanks were then china painted to give them the soft matted creme colored finish. They were then hand decorated including a detailed border pattern. In the case of the Hotelware, the pieces were left in the clear glazed state.

Occasionally, other colors of glaze were used instead of clear. At times, especially in the Carmen blank pieces, a boldly colored overglaze was utilized. The decal was applied as in the Old Ivory line. Often, the same decal was used as appears in one of the numbered patterns of Old Ivory. Other times, the same decal appeared in a different color. This situation was due to two factors. The color change may have been a choice, or may be influenced by the type of glazing used for the wares. The silicon base for the glaze as well as the metallic content can alter the color of a decal during firing.

Unlike the Old Ivory line, once the decal was applied, the only hand painting in the standard Hotelware was a single thin gold band, if any. This ware was meant to be affordable to commercial establishments whose volume (and breakage) was increased above the normal home use.

The pieces are marked with the single factory mark only, or the factory mark plus the blank name. On certain pieces, especially the more highly decorated, the artist mark appears. These patterns are never numbered.

The Hotelwares seem to be concentrated in the deep south surrounding Louisiana. Perhaps the port of entry of New Orleans specialized in that particular portion of the market.

The following is a collection of photographs illustrating the difference between blanks decorated in the Old Ivory style and identical blanks done in the Hotelware line. The side by side comparisons should eliminate the confusion that has arisen from the identification of these pieces.

Clairon

Demitasse pot

Eglantine

Sugar & creamer

Elysee

Chocolate pot

"Empire"

Plate

Carmen

Plate

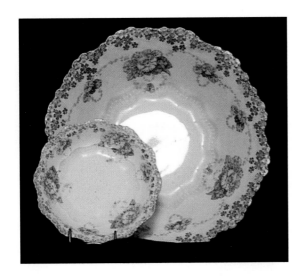

"Florette"

Serving bowl

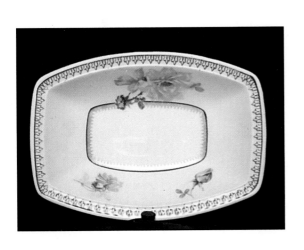

"Deco"

Oval vegetable

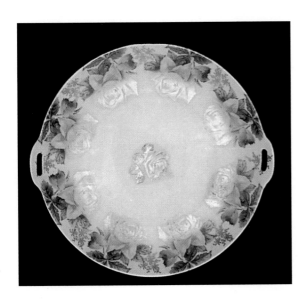

Alice

Cake plate

Mignon

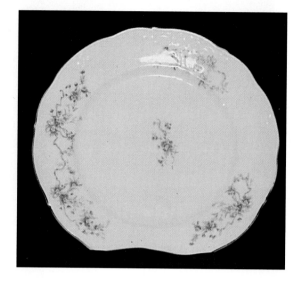

Dinner plate

Louis XVI

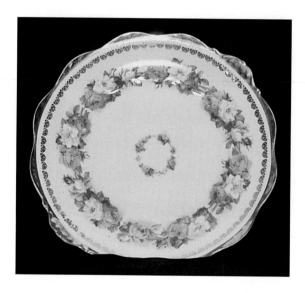

Plate

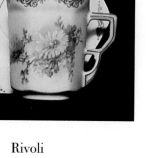

Rivoli

Chocolate cup

Etoile

Teacup & saucer

"Deco Variant"

Service creamer

"Alice Variant"

Platter

## *FANCY CLEAR GLAZED*

Within the Hotelware lines there were two divisions. The first was the standard series described above. The effort in producing this line was minimal compared to the Old Ivory wares. Therefore mass production (by hand) was facilitated.

On the other hand, the Ohme factory produced pieces of clear glazed porcelains without the matte finish of Old Ivory that were intricately hand decorated. These pieces must be isolated as a separate series of fancy clear glazed wares. The work in producing these pieces was not, in some cases, significantly different from that of Old Ivory wares and, thus, commands a higher value.

The method of differentiation between the Old Ivory pieces and the fancy clear glazed is a simple one, in theory. If the finish of the piece is china painted matte or pearlized, it is Old Ivory. If the finish is shiny glazed, over-sprayed, overglazed, or stamped, it is fancy clear glazed. In practice, the lines of demarcation are somewhat more blurred. Great care and debate has gone into placing these, often similar, pieces into the appropriate category.

For the collector, the Hotelware line is a more affordable version of Ohme porcelains. The fancy clear glazed line runs between **40%** and **50%** of the price of the comparable Old Ivory China, depending on intricacy of decoration. The plain Hotelware runs between **30%** and **40%** of the Old Ivory price, depending on availability.

There are some curious aspects to the choice of decal in the fancy clear glaze. The most noteworthy is Pamela. It is represented in the fancy clear glazed section, with aqua daisies on an Elysee blank and bearing the backstamp of "Pamela" (#C3). Oddly enough, a piece of Old Ivory, also on the Elysee blank, also with the same daisy decal, but in green and bearing the same backstamp of "Pamela" is found in the unidentified pattern section (#U20). How can a pattern of Old Ivory and of Hotelware be so similar and have the same backstamp?

Other examples include the decals which are used in the Hotelware and Old Ivory lines on the same pieces. Prime examples are the two fancy clear glaze patterns in Eglantine (#C15 & #C16). They are identical to the corresponding Old Ivory unidentified patterns (#U21 & #U22). Many more examples exist, however, these serve to be illustrative.

#C1 GLORIOSA
Blank: Alice
Type: Plate
Design: Large brown rose & butterfly

#C2
Blank: Florette
Type: Bowl
Design: creme & brown roses; green shading

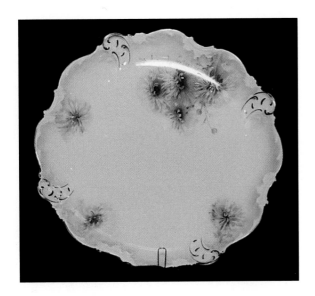

#C3 PAMELA
Blank: Elysee
Type: Coupe
Design: Aqua daisies; clear glaze Pamela

#C4 PERRUCHE
Blank: Elysee
Type: Plate
Design: White daisies blue shading

#C5
Blank: Elysee
Type: Plate
Design: White roses similar to #5

#C6
Blank: Elysee
Type: Shaving mug
Design: Rust hollyhock; green flowered border decal

#C7
Blank: Elysee
Type: Coupe
Design: Pastel hollyhocks; green flowered border decal

#C8
Blank: Carmen
Type: Cake plate
Design: Green open rose lavender shading

#C9
Blank: Carmen
Type: Pickle
Design: Pink roses; dark green shading

#C10
Blank: Carmen
Type: Plate
Design: White open rose; maroon shading

#C11
Blank: Carmen
Type: Plate
Design: White open rose; teal shading, pink border

#C12
Blank: Carmen
Type: Plate
Design: Red & white roses; gold background

#C13
Blank: Carmen
Type: Plate
Design: Pink lace work; bright pink background

#C14
Blank: Eglantine
Type: Coupe
Design: Small orange roses; peach shading, gray border

**#C15**
Blank: Eglantine
Type: Plate
Design: Lime green small flowers

**#C16**
Blank: Eglantine
Type: Biscuit
Design: Kelly green flowers on swags

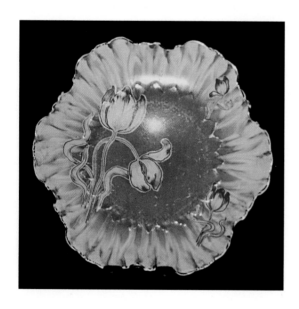

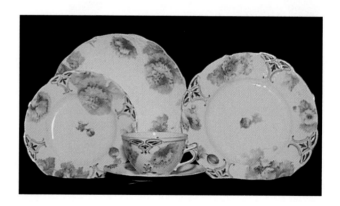

**#C17 PRINTEMPS III**
Blank: Eglantine
Type: Plate
Design: Red & yellow tulips; aqua background

**#C18**
Blank: Clairon
Type: Set
Design: Orange poppies; green scroll border

#C19
Blank: Clairon
Type: Plate
Design: Green open rose; red thin border

#C20
Blank: Clairon
Type: Chocolate
Design: Pink rose swags; gold scroll border

#C21
Blank: Clairon
Type: Plate
Design: Pink rose; light blue scroll border

#C22
Blank: Alice
Type: Plate
Design: Pink center rose; green shading

#C23
Blank: Alice
Type: Coupe
Design: Purple pansies; gold stamped border

#C24
Blank: Alice
Design: Three yellow roses; chocolate brown border

#C25
Blank: Alice
Type: Coupe
Design: Rust poppies; black shading

#C26
Blank: Alice
Type: Coupe
Design: Holly berries; thick fancy gold border

**#C27**
Blank: Alice
Type: Chocolate cup
Design: Red roses; broad red banding

**#C28**
Blank: Alice
Type: Coupe
Design: Gooseberries, carmel shading

**#C29**
Blank: Alice
Type: Cake plate
Design: Circle of roses; thick gold banded

**#C30**
Blank: Alice
Type: Bun tray
Design: Pink roses; thick fancy gold border

**#C31**
Blank: Alice
Type: Toureen
Design: Circle of pink roses

**#C32**
Blank: Alice
Type: Set
Design: Circle of pink roses; gold border

**#C33**
Blank: Alice
Type: Cup & saucer
Design: Pale pink roses blue-gray shading

**#C34**
Blank: Rivoli
Type: Cake plate
Design: Purple plums; thick gold border

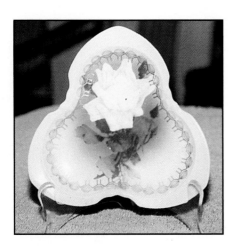

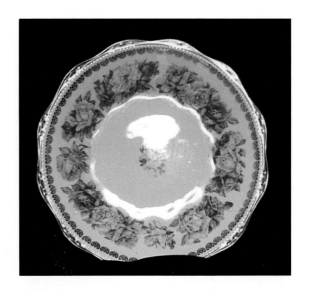

#C35
Blank: Rivoli
Type: Three lobed dish
Design: White center rose; blue shading

#C36
Blank: Louis XVI
Type: Plate
Design: Ring of red & white roses; gold border

## *HAND DECORATED*

Ohme factory blanks in clear glaze without any decal or decoration were made available for decoration outside the factory. This type of piece falls into two categories.

First, the factory decorated lines. These pieces are discussed in the previous section. Famous designers such as the Pickard and Tatler studios decorated Ohme blanks. Other companies copied the style of Ohme's Old Ivory China. Some even marketed their china with a backstamp of "Old Ivory." These examples will be discussed in the section of the book which follows, entitled "The Competitors."

The undecorated clear glazed blanks were also made available to the general public to china paint as they desired. The final products are not always inspiring, but they are individual. In addition, some artists dated their work, helping the researcher pinpoint a time frame for the production of that blank. Such examples are included in the following photographs.

A completely different situation is represented in the final two photographs. Here, pieces of the original Old Ivory set were lost or never originally obtained. The owner wished to match or fill out their china set. To that end, they purchased plain blanks from another company and decorated them to match their Old Ivory pattern. The work is skillful and laudable, and could fool the untrained eye. However, it is not Old Ivory and should not be considered so.

**GRAPES**
OHME blank: Clairon
Noteworthy as the work has been dated
**1905** by the artist. Workmanship is fair, at
best.

**STRAWBERRIES**
OHME blank: "Quadrille"
Noteworthy for the fine artistry and quality
workmanship.

**#73 DESIGN**
Bavarian blank
Good workmanship. Originally painted to
replace broken cups from a #73 Old Ivory
dinner set.

**#84 DESIGN**
Bavarian blank
Good workmanship. Probably painted to
replace broken plates from a #84 Old Ivory
dinner set.

# Competitors

The American market provided seemingly endless resources for the sale of goods from the European market. With the emergence of the *nouveau riche* in the United States around the turn of the century, a desire to copy the traditions of the aristocratic families was rampant. In the area of fine china, European was synonymous with elegance in the minds of these new pioneers of money.

To that end, the acquisition of a porcelain dinner set from a European manufacturer was both desirable and eagerly sought. The success of the Schlegelmilch or R.S. Prussia pieces is testimony to this passion.

The competition for this boundless American market was fierce. At that time, no patents on porcelain patterns or protection for the names existed in Europe. The manufacturers relied on an unwritten code of ethics not to copy existing china lines or pattern names. This code, like all others, was bound to be infringed upon, either overtly or covertly. Ohme, himself, patterened much of his china after the successful Haviland lines.

With the success of the Old Ivory line of china from the Ohme factory, several competitors sprang to copy the principles which opened the American market to them. The most visible calling card to success seemed to be the name of the china: Old Ivory. Hence, several manufacturers began to produce their own lines of china titled Old Ivory.

These china lines had no tangible relation to the Old Ivory China line produced by the Ohme factory. Some resemble in design the Ohme works and some bear no resemblance. In general, the quality of the porcelains and the workmanship in detailing is markedly inferior to the Ohme factory products. They do, however, provide an interesting mirror to the work of Hermann Ohme, and, perhaps, a more affordable collection to today's frugal consumer.

Many of the designs and patterns are attractive and some of the detailing is of a high standard.

Indeed, some of the shapes and designs are refreshing and inventive in their stlye and application. In many instances, the china lines could have stood on their own as prime examples of turn of the century porcelains. The availability and affordability of these wares makes them a tempting commodity. It is unfortunate that it was felt necessary to capitalize on the popularity of the name Old Ivory in labeling their works.

Certain of the patterns, particularly those of the first manufacturer listed, Three Crown China, have caused some confusion in the identification of pieces of Old Ivory China from the Ohme factory. Though of inferior manufacture and quality, the detailing is so similar to Ohme as to be confusing.

Even in America, the Old Ivory name was copied. Note the final examples in this section. Onandaga Pottery works came out with a line identified as Old Ivory. Lamberton China, though naming its line "Lamberton Ivory," produced china in such similar styling to Ohme china which is immediately evident.

Several well established collectors identify the competitor china lines as Old Ivory. While factual, this practice can be misleading to the novice or average collector. While these pieces are, indeed, Old Ivory and bear a backstamp that attests to that fact, they were not produced by the Ohme factory and bear no connection to the china lines discussed in this book. Their inclusion here is by way of clarification and edification.

This description is not to denegrate or degrade these china products of competing porcelain manufactories, but merely to separate them from the discussion of the Porcelain Manufactory Hermann Ohme and its product Old Ivory China.

The following is a pictorial guide to the most frequently located competitors marked with the Old Ivory backstamp.

### THREE CROWN CHINA (J.H.R. & CO.)
Roschutzer Porzellanfabrik Unger & Schilde Gmbh
Altenburg, Thuringer, Germany/Austria, 1881 – 1953

The Three Crown Old Ivory line produced most of the same pieces found in the Ohme factory products. Note the variety of pieces available within the Three Crown Old Ivory lines. Pictured on these pages alone are chocolate cups, rose bowl, cake plate, dinner plate, charger, bowl, mayonnaise, salt and pepper, jam jar, condensed milk container, celery, dresser tray, creamer, pickle dish, water pitcher, milk pitcher, chocolate pot, cracker jar, syrup pitcher, candy dish, scuttle, cider cups, powder jar, and hair receiver. This does not include the myriad of plates, bowls, cups and saucers, and other common pieces available to the collector. These pieces are far more reasonably priced than corresponding Ohme pieces, as would be expected due to the inferior workmanship. However, they do form an attractive and affordable (and useable) collection.

The Roschutzer factory produced a wide variety of Old Ivory pieces. The marks varied greatly among the wares. Although, the marks may have importance in dating the production, there is little evidence to document any time scale.

The Three Crown patterns most closely resemble Old Ivory China produced in the Hermann Ohme factory in style and decoration. However, the quality of the wares is far inferior. The main blank style has been referred to as the "Shamrock Border" for obvious reasons. The three most common designs for the main line of Old Ivory from this company were

1. A brown open rose similar to the #11 rose of Ohme.
2. A pink rose somewhat similar to the #16 rose of Ohme.
3. A yellow rose reminiscent of the #200 rose of Ohme.
4. A pink thistle pattern utilizing the identical decal as those used by the K. Steinmann factory.

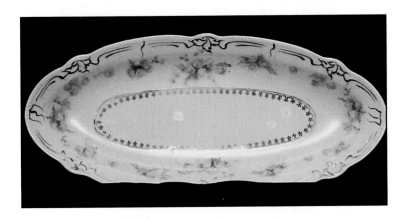

Three Crown also produced a line of "Thistle-ware" which is very popular with collectors. There are collectors who specialize exclusively in this decorative style. Intriguingly, the flower design and decal is identical to that used by K. Steinmann Company of Tiefenfurth in their "Thistle-ware." However, the blank is significantly different. The edge has a raised beadwork punctuated with large leaf-like scrolls. Below the beadwork are thin bands of applied gold. Please note comparison under K. Steinmann Company. The line of "Thistle-ware" from Three Crown China does not appear to be as plentiful as the version marketed by K. Steinmann Company.

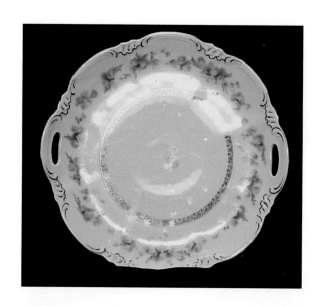

The sugar and creamer, along with the charger pictured at the top left were marked with the name Eagle China rather than Three Crown China. However, they bear the same backstamp (J.H.R. & Co.) as the cake plate on the top right. This cake plate has the same mold as the Three Crown China pieces, forming the link of the two names under the same company. As corroborative evidence, the filigree of the sugar and creamer matches the filigree of the Three Crown "Thistle-ware."

The pieces on this page are the only examples found bearing the marks of J.H.R. & Co. Those bearing the black circle mark have the country of origin listed as Austria, while the ones bearing the reddish-brown mark originate in Germany. The significance of this distinction is probably similar to that of the Ohme factory country of origin marks. The area of Thuringer changed from Austria to Germany during the period of operation of the factory. The pieces bear the ever-popular thistle pattern, however, workmanship is crude.

## STRIEGAUER PORCELAIN FACTORY
### Stanowitz, Silesia, Germany, 1873 – 1927

The St. P.M. line of Striegauer porcelain is very close to the Ohme factory product in both style and design. Though the craftsmanship is slightly inferior to traditional Old Ivory, it is an attractive and reasonable substitute. This Old Ivory came in two border designs. The first was a series of crossed leaves. There were two patterns used for this border design: a white wild rose and red small roses. The second border design was a thin filigreed band punctuated at the four stations of the clock by a fleur de lis-type scroll. Apparently, only one pattern used for this border design: a red poppy.

Although "La Touraine" Old Ivory is an attractive mold and pattern, it bears little resemblance to Ohme factory products in either style or design. The phrase "La Touraine" may refer to the blank design, which would include the yellow rose designed sugar and creamer in the lower right-hand corner; or it may refer to the lily of the valley decal used. In this case, the sugar and creamer (as well as the cake plate from the preceding page) are of a different pattern. No evidence has surfaced to this point to support either theorum.

## K. STEINMANN COMPANY
Tiefenfurth, Silesia, Germany, 1868 – 1938

The marks are four in number. The first is a fusiform shaped mark notably similar to the contemporary E. Schlegelmilch mark pictured below. The second and third marks are the same stylized crown mark, but in two colors: red and blue. The third mark is an oddly shaped crown perched above the cross of a large "X," similar to the early Ohme X mark.

It now appears that this factory preferred to mimic existing and successful lines of chinas rather than to create its own original and new designs.

*Erdmann Schlegelmilch*
*Suhl, 1891 – 1938*

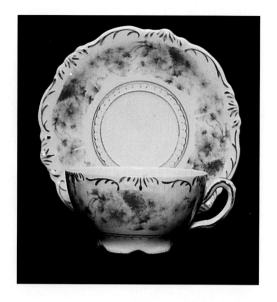

There were three major blank designs utilized. The first had a lacy border with ovoid recesses at the four quarters. The two patterns used for this blank were purple sprays and red roses. The second blank was a plain, lightly ruffled edge accented with gold. The patterns for this blank were red and pink roses, yellow daisies, and thistle. The third blank was similar to Three Crown China, but with three shamrocks at each quarter instead of one. Only one pattern found: white and pink open roses. There have also been several other blank styles located. These are included on page **202**.

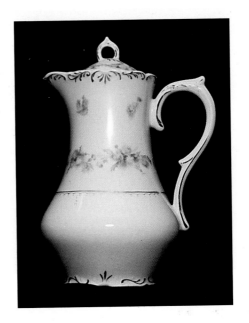

Though prolific in the number of china pieces exported, the line suffers from a lack of quality workmanship. The design and styling bear little resemblance to the Old Ivory produced in the Hermann Ohme factory. This is, perhaps, the most inferior quality of the competitor lines.

This company also produced a line of "Thistle-ware" popular with collectors today. There seems to be a greater number of pieces than the Three Crown China counterpart. However, the decal is exactly the same. Please see Three Crown China.

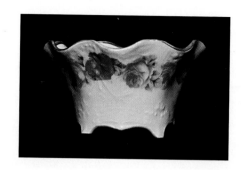

## C. TIELSCH & COMPANY
Altwasser, Silesia, Germany, 1875 - 1935

As with the St. P.M. line of Striegau, the Old Ivory China produced by Tielsch was a quality line bearing good design and artistic merit. Its style is very similar to the Ohme Factory products and the workmanship is almost comparable. All in all, it is a fine alternative to the genuine article. Only one common blank has been found. It is usually decorated with a ring of single roses in pink and yellow alternating with an acanthus leaf design. Of note is a single piece of C.T. pictured in the middle photo above. The design is extremely close to Ohme Old Ivory, however, its bold design belies the similarity.

**203**

## TETTAU PORCELAIN FACTORY
### Tettau, Bavaria, Germany, 1916 – present

### ROYAL BAYREUTH PORCELAIN

Though identified as Old Ivory, the back-stamp is simply hand-painted Ivory. Only one mark was utilized for this line. One cannot argue that the quality and craftsmanship of this china is comparable to Ohme's. The china is fine, light and airy. The pierce carving or cutwork of the edges adds greatly to its charm and appeal. The designs are of superior quality and executed skillfully. However, the figures are more stylized and ponderous and the design bears no resemblance to Hermann Ohme's Ivory.

UNKNOWN CHINA MANUFACTURER
Germany

The styling and design of this porcelain is bold and distinctive. The workmanship is reasonable, though not on a par with the Ohme factory product. No factory name has been found to date.

*THE AMERICAN COUSINS*

Plate
open coach pattern

ONANDAGA POTTERY
COMPANY
Syracuse, New York, USA,
1871 – ?

LAMBERTVILLE CHINA
COMPANY
Lambertville, Pennsylvania,
USA 19??

Cream soup bowl
Rita Maria pattern

# Price Guide

The following is a rough price guide for Old Ivory China. It was necessary to quote a range of prices due to the variability between the value of different pattern numbers and blank styles, as well as the geographic differences in availability and, thus, price of individual pieces.

There are several key notes when using this table.

**The prices quoted are for mint quality examples:**

Worn gold filigree diminishes value by 10 – 25%.

Please note that certain patterns have a proclivity toward worn gold. In these patterns only, gold wear is acceptable. Many collectors do not wish to purchase any Old Ivory China that does not have perfect gold filigree.

Minor damage diminishes value by 25% or more.

Minor damage refers to such things as minor rim flakes. Small chips in obscure areas, etc.

Major damage diminishes value by a minimum of 50%.

Please note that Old Ivory collectors in general are quite particular as to the quality of a piece. What might be viewed as minor damage in another china company's product is viewed as major damage to the Old Ivory enthusiast. Many collectors will only consider perfect examples.

Lidless items command only between 25% and 50% of the price of the complete item. Damaged lids usually decrease price by 20 – 40% dependent on extent and type of damage.

**Holly pieces command 25 – 50% above the price range as do some of the rarer pattern numbers.**

**Geographic location influences prices.**

Each region has its own selection of readily accessible pattern numbers or types. Certain pieces tend to show up in only one area. Eg.: Pacific Northwest, New England, Midwest, or South. Adjustments in price scale must be made to accomodate for these differences in supply.

Maine, which has the largest supply of Old Ivory available tends to command a slightly lesser price locally; usually 5 – 10% less than the listed price.

**Hotelware utilizes the same comparisons between pieces, however, the scale is far less. The price guide for hotelware is two-fold.**

Fancy decorated ware (more than just a decal and a single band of gold trim) commands 40 – 50% of corresponding pieces of Old Ivory.

Standard Hotelware (plain decal and gold trim without hand decorating) commands only 25% of corresponding pieces of Old Ivory.

| ITEM | SIZE (width) | PRICE RANGE |
|---|---|---|
| **Plates:** | | |
| Dinner Plate | 9½" or 10" | $200.00 – 275.00 |
| Luncheon Plate | 8½" | $50.00 – 95.00 |
| Salad Plate | 7½" | $40.00 – 85.00 |
| Bread and Butter Plate | 7" | $30.00 – 75.00 |
| Dessert Plate | 6" | $25.00 – 55.00 |
| Coupe Plate | 9½" or 10" | $200.00 – 300.00 |
| Coupe Plate | 8½" | $100.00 – 200.00 |
| Coupe Plate | 7¾" | $75.00 – 95.00 |
| Coupe Plate | 6¼" | $50.00 – 75.00 |

| ITEM | SIZE (width) | PRICE RANGE |
|---|---|---|
| Open Handled | | |
| Cake Plate | 10" or 11" | $100.00 – 195.00 |
| Charger (Chop Plate) | 13" | $200.00 – 400.00 |
| Soup Plate | 10" | $175.00 – 200.00 |
| Butter Pat | 3¼" | $100.00 – 150.00 |
| **Platters:** | | |
| Platter | 28" | $800.00 – 1000.00 |
| Platter (fish) | 23" | $800.00 – 1000.00 |
| Platter | 21" | $500.00 – 600.00 |
| Platter | 16½" | $300.00 – 400.00 |

| ITEM | SIZE (width) | PRICE RANGE | ITEM | SIZE (width) | PRICE RANGE |
|---|---|---|---|---|---|
| Platter | 13½" | $200.00 – 300.00 | Coffee Pot | 9" tall | $500.00 – 700.00 |
| Platter | 11½" | $100.00 – 200.00 | Teapot | 8½" tall | $400.00 – 600.00 |
| **Round Bowls:** | | | Demi Pot | 7½" tall | $400.00 – 600.00 |
| Round Bowl | 9" or 10" | $100.00 – 175.00 | Bisquit or Cracker Jar | 8" tall | $400.00 – 600.00 |
| Soup Bowl | 7½" | $125.00 – 175.00 | Sugar Bowl | 5½" tal | $60.00 – 140.00 |
| Cereal Bowl | 6½" | $50.00 – 85.00 | Service Sugar Bowl | 6" tall | $175.00 – 350.00 |
| Oatmeal Bowl | 6½" | $55.00 – 95.00 | Creamer | 3½" tall | $60.00 – 110.00 |
| Sauce Bowl | 5½" | $25.00 – 45.00 | Service Creamer | 5½" tall | $150.00 – 325.00 |
| Small Berry Bowl | 5" | $25.00 – 45.00 | Spooner | 4" tall | $275.00 – 400.00 |
| Footed Bowl | 6" | $100.00 – 150.00 | Waste or Oyster Bowl | 5" | $175.00 – 225.00 |
| Ice Cream Bowl | 10" | $125.00 – 195.00 | Tea Tray | 21" | $800.00 – 1,000.00 |
| Nappy | 6½" | $100.00 – 175.00 | Tea Tile | 6" | $100.00 – 175.00 |
| **Oblong Bowls:** | | | Toothpick Holder | 2¼5" tall | $200.00 – 250.00 |
| Oval Vegetable Bowl | 9½" | $125.00 – 185.00 | Jam Jar | 3½" tall | $200.00 – 300.00 |
| Large Oval Center Bowl | 11" | $650.00 – 850.00 | Mustard Pot | 3¾" tall | $175.00 – 275.00 |
| Celery Dish | 11¼" | $100.00 – 195.00 | **Serving Dishes:** | | |
| Pickle Dish | 8½" | $75.00 – 100.00 | Covered Vegetable (round) | 10½" | $400.00 – 800.00 |
| Olive Dish | 6½" | $65.00 – 85.00 | Covered Vegetable (oval) | 10½" | $400.00 – 800.00 |
| Porringer | 6¼" | $75.00 – 125.00 | Soup Toureen | 13" | $1,800.00 – 2,500.00 |
| Lay Down Spooner | 8¼" | $100.00 – 150.00 | Covered Butter Dish | | |
| Toast & Tea Set | 8¼"+3" | $175.00 – 250.00 | (with insert) | 7½" | $700.00 – 900.00 |
| Ladle Holder | 6½" | $200.00 – 250.00 | Covered Cheese Dish* | 9½" | |
| Bun Tray | 12" | $200.00 – 250.00 | Small Covered Sauce Boat | 8½" | $900.00 – 1,200.00 |
| Bun Tray | 10" | $175.00 – 225.00 | Gravy Boat | 8½" | $800.00 – 1,000.00 |
| Bun Tray | 8" | $150.00 – 200.00 | Mayonnaise & Underplate | 6½" | $150.00 – 250.00 |
| Handled Basket | 8" | $200.00 – 400.00 | Ramakin & | | |
| Three Lobed Dish | 8½" | $100.00 – 175.00 | Underplate | 4¼"+5" | $400.00 – 600.00 |
| Three Lobed Dish | 7¼" | $75.00 – 125.00 | Tazza or Cake Stand | 9" | $250.00 – 400.00 |
| Three Lobed Dish | 6" | $50.00 – 95.00 | Compote | 9" | $300.00 – 500.00 |
| Candy Dish (bow tie shaped) | 8" | $100.00 – 185.00 | Open Salt (individual)* | | |
| Bone Dish (crescent shaped) | | $400.00 – 600.00 | Salt & Pepper | | |
| **Cups:** | | | Shakers | 2¾" (pair) | $100.00 – 150.00 |
| Coffee Cup & Saucer | 3½" | $70.00 – 90.00 | Muffineer or Sugar Shaker | | $300.00 – 400.00 |
| Tea Cup & Saucer | 3¼" | $65.00 – 85.00 | Water Pitcher | 8" tall | $800.00 – 1,100.00 |
| 5-o'clock Tea Cup & Saucer | 3" | $65.00 – 85.00 | Center Handle | | |
| Demitasse Cup & Saucer | 2½" | $85.00 – 115.00 | Double Server* | 12" | |
| Chocolate Cup & Saucer | 2¼" | $75.00 – 95.00 | **Dresser Sets:** | | |
| Bouillon Cup & Saucer | 3½" | $175.00 – 250.00 | Dresser Tray | 12½" | $125.00 – 225.00 |
| Cider Cup & Saucer | 3" | $250.00 – 350.00 | Dresser Tray | 11½" | $100.00 – 200.00 |
| Moustache Cup & Saucer | 3½" | $300.00 – 400.00 | Hat Pin Holder* | | |
| Shaving Mug | 3¼" | $550.00 – 1200.00 | Powder Jar (lidded) | | $200.00 – 350.00 |
| Egg Cup | 2½" | $400.00 – 550.00 | Covered Trinket | 3" | $300.00 – 600.00 |
| Chowder Cup* | 4" | | Hair Receiver | | $200.00 – 350.00 |
| **Pots/Tea Sets:** | | | Toothbrush Holder | 4" tall | $175.00 – 275.00 |
| Chocolate Pot | 9½" tall | $250.00 – 450.00 | Vase | Variable | $200.00 – 500.00 |

\* indicates that there are not enough samples to formulate a price range.

# Bibliography

*China Decorator, The*. Katherine Cline. Volume VIII number 1, January, 1963.

*China Decorator, The*. Katherine Cline. Volume VIII number 6, June, 1963.

*China Decorator, The*. Katherine Cline on Painting Flowers and Fruits. Volume XV number 1, July, 1970.

Gilbert, Martin - editor. *Recent Historical Atlas*. New York: McMillan Publishers , 1969.

Katz-Foerstner, A. *Handbuch der Deutschen Wirtschaft*, Schlesien. Berlin: Halensee, 1929.

Keil, Georg. *Das Niederschlesische Industriegebiet*. Seine Entwicklung und Notlage. Berlin: Volk und Reich Verlag, 1935

Kohrer, E. *Niederschlesien seine Entwicklung und seine Zukunft*. Berlin: Deursche Stadt, 1923.

Malzenstw, Ksiega. *Standes Amt Waldenburg. Heirats - Haupt Register*. Archiwum Panstwowe we Wroclawiu, 1995.

McNally, Rand - editor. *Historical Atlas of the World*. New York: Rand McNally, 1981.

Neuen Tageblatt. *Das Ende der Ohmeschen Fabrik*. April 18 / 19, 1936.

Nowak, L.A. *Kunstgewerbe in Schlesien 1900 – 1945*. Schlesein- Kunst Wissenschaft Volkskunde Wurzburg, 1992.

Robaszynnska, Malgorzata. *Ceramika w zbiorach Muzeum Okregowego w Walbrzychu*. Walbrzych, 1988.

Rontgen, Robert E. *Marks on German, Bohemian and Austrian Porcelain - 1710 to the Present*. Pennsylvania: Schiffer Publishing Ltd., 1981.

Schweidnitz 1889. *Jahres-Bericht der Handelskammer zu Schweidnits fur das jahr 1888*. Wroclaw: University of Wroclaw, 1995.

Schweidnitz 1892. *Jahres-Bericht der Handelskammer zu Schweidnits fur das jahr 1891*. Wroclaw: University of Wroclaw, 1995.

Schweidnitz 1895. *Jahres-Bericht der Handelskammer zu Schweidnits fur das jahr 1894*. Wroclaw: University of Wroclaw, 1995.

Siess-Krzyszkowski, Stanislaw. *Znaki Firmowe fabryk porcelany i fajansu na Slasku*, w Wielkopolsce i na Pomorzu od roku 1795 do dnia dzisiejszego. Walbrzych, 1995.

Starzewska, Maria. *Z dziejow ceramiki na Slasku*. Wroclaw: Dolnoslaskei Towarzystwo Spoleczno- Kulturalne, 1977.

Starzewska, Maria; Jezewska, Maria. *Slaska porcelana*. Wroclaw: Krajowa Agencja Wydawnicza, 1987.

Zuhlsdorff, Dieter. Marken Lexikon: *porzellan und keramik report 1885 – 1935*. Stuttgart: Arnoldsche, 1990.